AF756939

Research, Development and Innovation in the Creative Industries

What does effective research and development look like in the creative industries and how might it lead to successful innovation? This book is an answer to that question.

Building upon place-based creative industry research, the book focuses on evidence from the media sector, while encompassing a range of creative practices, from digital tourism to dance. Leveraging unique empirical data from the Welsh creative industries, the authors map a series of pathways for creative businesses. In so doing, the book offers new frameworks for assessing innovative practice and highlights options for tailored institutional funding.

Channelling research insights, this shortform book helps researchers, policy-makers and reflective practitioners to understand how to deliver effective strategies for the creative sector.

Ruxandra Lupu is Marie Curie Fellow at the University of Cyprus.

Marlen Komorowski is Senior Research Fellow of Media Cymru at JOMEC, Cardiff University, Senior Researcher at imec – SMIT – VUB and Guest Professor for European Media Markets at Vrije Universiteit Brussels.

Justin Lewis is Professor of Communication and Creative Industries at Cardiff University, UK, and Director of Media Cymru.

Máté Miklos Fodor is Associate Professor of Economics at the Project Management Institute of Satbayev University, Almaty, Kazakhstan.

Aliya Turegeldinova is Head of Management and mathematical economics department of Kazakh National Research Technical University named after K. I. Satpayev, Candidate of Economic Sciences, PhD, Almaty, Kazakhstan.

Meiram Begentayev is Rector of Kazakh National Research Technical University named after K. I. Satpayev, Doctor of economic sciences, associate professor, Almaty, Kazakhstan.

Routledge Focus on the Global Creative Economy
Series Editor: Aleksandar Brkić, *Goldsmiths, University of London, UK*

This innovative Shortform book series aims to provoke and inspire new ways of thinking, new interpretations, emerging research, and insights from different fields. In rethinking the relationship of creative economies and societies beyond the traditional frameworks, the series is intentionally inclusive. Featuring diverse voices from around the world, books in the series bridge scholarship and practice across arts and cultural management, the creative industries and the global creative economy.

Global Crisis and the Creative Industries
Analysing the Impact of the Covid-19 Pandemic
Ryan Daniel

Creative Economy and Sustainable Development
The Context of Indian Handicrafts
Madhura Dutta

Music Artist Managers
Remuneration and Retention in the Popular Music Business
Guy Morrow

Climate Change and the Creative Economy in India
Disadvantaged, Disturbed and Dislocated Indian Weavers
Pragya Sharma

Research, Development and Innovation in the Creative Industries
Reframing Our Understanding of the Creative Economy
Ruxandra Lupu, Marlen Komorowski, Justin Lewis and Máté Miklos Fodor

For more information about this series, please visit: www.routledge.com/Routledge-Focus-on-the-Global-Creative-Economy/book-series/RFGCE

Research, Development and Innovation in the Creative Industries

Reframing Our Understanding of the Creative Economy

Ruxandra Lupu, Marlen Komorowski, Justin Lewis and Máté Miklos Fodor

Routledge
Taylor & Francis Group
LONDON AND NEW YORK

First published 2025
by Routledge
4 Park Square, Milton Park, Abingdon, Oxon OX14 4RN

and by Routledge
605 Third Avenue, New York, NY 10158

Routledge is an imprint of the Taylor & Francis Group, an informa business

© 2025 Ruxandra Lupu, Marlen Komorowski, Justin Lewis and Máté Miklos Fodor

The right of Ruxandra Lupu, Marlen Komorowski, Justin Lewis and Máté Miklos Fodor to be identified as authors of this work has been asserted in accordance with sections 77 and 78 of the Copyright, Designs and Patents Act 1988.

The Open Access version of this book, available at www.taylorfrancis.com, has been made available under a Creative Commons Attribution-Non Commercial-No Derivatives (CC-BY-NC-ND) 4.0 license.

Any third party material in this book is not included in the OA Creative Commons license, unless indicated otherwise in a credit line to the material. Please direct any permissions enquiries to the original rightsholder.

Trademark notice: Product or corporate names may be trademarks or registered trademarks, and are used only for identification and explanation without intent to infringe.

British Library Cataloguing-in-Publication Data
A catalogue record for this book is available from the British Library

ISBN: 978-1-032-77202-8 (hbk)
ISBN: 978-1-032-77206-6 (pbk)
ISBN: 978-1-003-48180-5 (ebk)

DOI: 10.4324/9781003481805

Typeset in Times New Roman
by SPi Technologies India Pvt Ltd (Straive)

This work was supported by the Arts and Humanities Research Council [AH/S002790/1].

Arts and
Humanities
Research Council

Contents

Figures

Tables

Preface

The authors of this book, from Cardiff University's Centre for the Creative Economy, are part of a sustained programme of creative industries research, development and innovation (R,D&I) in Wales. The book documents and analyses the first main stage of this work – the Clwstwr project (2018–2022) – part of the Creative Industries Cluster Programme (CICP), the United Kingdom (UK) government's first concerted investment in creative industries R,D&I, delivered through the Arts and Humanities Research Council (AHRC).

The CICP programme broke new ground, applying the tools of R,D&I – largely developed in scientific and technological sectors – to the creative industries across the UK. Like any new initiative, it was experimental and iterative – a textbook example of action research. Creating a new innovation ecosystem for industries largely unfamiliar with R,D&I involved a simultaneous process of development and assessment. We developed approaches, curated the R,D&I that followed and assessed our processes. We then changed our approach in response to this assessment, curating a new round of R,D&I, assessing what worked, what didn't and so on.

The learning curve was steep for all concerned. Towards the end of Clwstwr, we (the Centre for the Creative Economy) were able to use this learning to become the first humanities/social sciences project to bid successfully to UK Research and Innovation's (UKRI) flagship Strength in Places Fund (SIPF – designed to increase place-based productivity and growth). This has enabled us to continue to develop the R,D&I ecosystem developed through Clwstwr – now refocused as Media Cymru (2022–2026).

The success of Clwstwr and the CICP programme, as evidenced by the recent evaluation commissioned by AHRC,[1] clearly signals to policy makers that the creative industries should be part of the UK's industrial strategy (at the time of writing, in late 2024, the AHRC announced the second wave of the CICP programme, while the new UK government has included the creative industries as one of its eight key growth sectors). But we have also learnt that this is not a simple case of extending traditional R,D&I

models to (generally small-scale) creative organisations and businesses. This is a sector made up of small and micro businesses that need support at an ecosystem – rather than at an individual or corporate level. It needs programmes tailored to creative industries needs and practices.

In this book, we look back across the Clwstwr programme to offer a considered reflection of what these might look like. It informs our own work through Media Cymru, but we hope it will also inform future policy and practice in this area.

Note

1 BOP consulting and Frontier Economics (2024) Evaluation of the Creative Industries Clusters Programme, Arts and Humanities Research Council, Accessible online at: https://www.ukri.org/publications/evaluation-of-the-creative-industries-clusters-programme/.

Acknowledgements

Our work, throughout, has involved working with hundreds of creative businesses, freelancers and other stakeholders, and included many collaborations and co-creations. There are, as a consequence, many people to thank, beginning with the many creative companies that took part in Clwstwr, with whom we have learnt so much, and whose stories fill the pages that follow.

We would also like to thank: the AHRC and Welsh Government – especially Helen Weedon and Paul Osbaldeston – for their positivity, flexibility and support throughout; our colleagues at the University of South Wales (USW) and Cardiff Metropolitan – especially Andy Walters and Jo Ward, who were integral to developing an R&D process for creative businesses; the Clwstwr Management Team – Ruth Cayford, Jarred Evans, Miguela Gonzalez, Rich Hurford, Gareth Jones, Lisa Matthew Jones, Ruth McElroy, Robin Moore and Sara Pepper, supported brilliantly by Angie Dutton; the Clwstwr Steering Board led by Geraint Talfan Davies and Ann Beynon; our many colleagues at Cardiff University, especially Ian Hargreaves and David Dunkley Gyimah.

Finally, a huge thanks to all our very special colleagues in the Clwstwr delivery team – Alma Abby, Laolu Alatise, Steve Davies, Sally Griffiths, Beca Harries, Gavin Johnson, Kayleigh McLeod, Greg Mothersdale, Becca Palmer, Adam Partridge, Sara Pepper and Lee Walters. They have lived and breathed this work with us.

Introduction

This book represents one of the few large-scale empirical studies of how the creative industries engage with an innovation ecosystem. It offers a comprehensive and holistic analysis of the role of research, development and innovation (R,D&I) within the creative industries and new ways to understand the role and impact of the creative economy.

We use a multidimensional conceptual positioning to understand the functioning of R,D&I in the creative industries. First, the epistemological and historical foundations of the study set the basis for understanding the evolution of the concept of creative industries, by tracing its emergence and evolution in the context of policy and creative industries development. Second, the perceptual and empirical lens deployed to analyse the way creative businesses look at the concept of R,D&I, provides an assessment of the value to creatives. Third, a structural and typological approach deployed for the analysis of collected data, enables the definition of forms of classification for R&D-based innovation. Finally, we use a strategic and future-oriented lens to determine optimal R&D support levels required for thriving and innovative creative industries.

Chapter 1 traces the conceptual and material rise of the creative industries, towards a broad understanding of a creative economy that incorporates both art and culture and the more commercial creative sectors. Despite the persistence of a fragmented policy framework that compartmentalises the creative industries under traditional cultural headings, this move has led to the creative industries becoming part of industrial strategies, with the subsequent incorporation of the use of R&D within the CCIs. The chapter looks at the critical landscape of debates around the creative industries, much of which questions the 'economic turn' associated with a creative industries approach.

Chapter 2 highlights the need for a closer assessment of R,D&I practices within creative companies from the perspective of creative businesses. It highlights the need to assess more closely the ways in which creative businesses perceive R&D processes through multiple perspectives: analysing the value assigned to R&D, while assessing the specific characteristics of R&D processes within the creative industries. It deploys a mixed-method lens that brings to light the values assigned to R&D (novelty, time-effectiveness, market readiness) as well as the perceptual characteristics of R&D within the creative industries.

Chapter 3 looks at how R&D-based typologies of innovation can successfully feed into the work of researchers, policymakers and practitioners. We propose a classification model that aims to overcome the challenges posed by existing models (e.g. a reliance on linear forms of novelty, exclusively technocratic approaches, from language to forms of measurement). The model establishes two core axes of measurement: the direction of R&D and the degree of learning throughout the R&D process. These give rise to four distinct archetypes of R&D-driven innovation within the creative industries: (1) technocratic, (2) incremental, (3) conceptualising and (4) disrupting, all of which are necessary and form a variegated and heterogenous innovation landscape needed for thriving creative industries.

Chapter 4 looks at the range of support mechanisms provided by the Clwstwr programme and explores the optimal levels and timing of support required to undertake R&D in the creative industries. The methodology consists of applying statistical and econometric analysis on data extracted through ex-post evaluations and interviews, using a longitudinal method to trace satisfaction and success throughout the R&D journey. Key findings underscore the importance of a balanced support approach, tailored to the specific needs of projects. In doing so, it provides useful guidelines for successful future funding programmes in the creative industries.

In Chapter 5, we draw the main conclusions of the study, outlining a roadmap for understanding, conceptualising and supporting the adoption of R,D&I as a precondition for thriving creative industries.

Chapters are designed both as a holistic study and as a modular structure that enables selective reading. The book is a resource for students, researchers, policy makers and creative businesses.

1 The cultural, economic and social value of the creative industries

Justin Lewis

A brief history of creative industries policy

During the first half of the 20th century, culture became an industry. The growth of cultural forms like popular music, radio, cinema and the press became part of – and subject to the terms of – industrial production. Frankfurt School scholars Theodor Adorno and Max Horkheimer, writing in response to the mechanisation of cultural objects in pursuit of mass markets, were among the first to coin the term 'the culture industry' (Adorno & Horkheimer, 1947). They were writing against the backdrop of what they saw as the twin dystopias of the rise of fascism across Europe and the hyper-commercialisation of culture in the United States (US).

Not surprisingly, the appropriation of 'mass culture' for propaganda and profit created a widespread sense of foreboding. Films like Leni Riefenstahl's *Triumph of the Will* injected fascist iconography with cinematic flair, while the hyper-commercial model of the US television industry produced a cultural landscape that would famously be described (by John F. Kennedy's Federal Communications Commissioner, Newton Minow) as 'a vast wasteland'. Caught between these two versions of mass culture, the Frankfurt School provided a famously pessimistic commentary on the industrialisation of cultural production.

Today, they are best known for their attack on the formulaic limits of capitalist logic on mass cultural forms. They saw cultural, social and economic imperatives pulling in different directions and argued that the logic of the marketplace – with its preference for lowest common denominator, consumerist and formulaic cultural forms – did not always create positive social or cultural outcomes. But some of the Frankfurt School's early work – notably Walter Benjamin (in his 1935 essay, *The Work of Art in the Age of Mechanical Reproduction*) – was more optimistic, deconstructing the aesthetics of fascism while celebrating the more democratic creative potential of popular cultural genres like film.

Benjamin's appeal to a Brechtian, progressive form of mass culture – in which the workings of history are revealed in popular narratives – was,

DOI: 10.4324/9781003481805-1
This chapter has been made available under a CC BY-NC-ND 4.0 license.

perhaps, too hopeful for its time. Today, the Frankfurt School is more likely to be associated with Adorno and Horkeimer's gloomier vision of the industrialisation of culture. While Adorno and Horkeimer's critique was radical in some ways – alongside other critics of consumer capitalism, such as Vance Packard and J.K. Galbraith (Lewis, 1990) – like most of their contemporaries they assumed a traditional dichotomy between culture and commerce. This dichotomy became enshrined in a policy distinction between publicly funded cultural forms – free from commerce and seen as having high cultural value – and more commercial, popular culture, generally regarded as having lower cultural value.

This distinction was promoted by cultural arbiters from a range of political perspectives – in the UK from the influential literary critic FR Leavis to the BBC's first Director General, Lord John Reith. While both Leavis and Reith were driven by democratic instincts, they assumed it was the educated middle classes who were best equipped to understand cultural value and to distinguish between 'good' and 'bad' forms of creativity. They wanted to widen access to 'good culture' while keeping a tight hold on the forms it might take. Cultural value became, almost by definition, a counterpart to popular taste: a distinction that was quickly embedded in public policy, whether through Reithian models of public service broadcasting or public funding of the arts (Lewis, 1990).

The cultural theorist Raymond Williams, alongside the Birmingham Centre for Contemporary Cultural Studies (founded by Stuart Hall and Richard Hoggart in 1964), questioned the value system behind this distinction. They argued for a much broader, more inclusive notion of culture and creativity, one that included popular as well as 'high' culture. They developed an idea of culture and creativity based on most people's lived experiences. Cultural activity could not be reduced to an appreciation of a literary canon, fine art or classical music.

Pierre Bourdieu's famous work, *Distinction* (2018), added sociological weight to this more inclusive cultural terrain. *Distinction* used survey data to explore how notions of cultural legitimacy were not based on a set of objective truths. Rather, they were bound up with – and expressions of – social class. Bourdieu argued that this distinction created a system of public legitimation that preserved and protected the tastes of the more privileged sections of society– those who possessed what Bourdieu called 'cultural capital'.

These critiques of the traditional cultural value system – alongside the prodigious growth and ubiquity of the cultural industries themselves – began to change the way we understood art, culture and creativity. By the 1980s the academy was no longer a space reserved for the study and legitimation of the high arts. The growth of the social sciences made it untenable to focus attention exclusively on cultural forms – such as literature, fine art and classical music – that were far less widely enjoyed than most forms of popular culture. If high culture eluded large sections of society, popular culture had, for most people, become an integral part of everyday life. This laid the ground for the beginnings of a policy shift. For all its democratic desires, traditional arts funding was regressive, in effect (if not in intent) subsidising entertainment for more privileged sections of society (Lewis, 1990).

In the 1980s the Greater London Council (GLC) alongside the Great London Enterprise Board (GLEB) began to imagine what a broader, more democratic cultural policy might look like. GLEB's work was led by Geoff Mulgan and Ken Worpole, whose 1986 book, *Saturday Night and Sunday Morning*, laid out a move away from the more exclusive idea of 'the arts' towards the broader notion of 'the creative industries'. They asked how policy interventions – supporting innovative independent record labels for example – might have positive impacts across this much broader cultural space.

The notion of the 'creative industries' and the importance of popular culture reverberated through the academy, with the growth of cultural studies, media studies and other related disciplines, alongside a broader disciplinary recognition of the importance of the media and creative industries to democratic institutions and everyday life. But the abolition of the GLC, combined with local government cutbacks in cultural funding across the UK, stalled the rise of more sustained creative industries initiatives. On the other side of the world, Paul Keating's Australian Government, alongside a growing Australian cultural industries literature, picked up the creative industries theme. The *Creative Nation* report, published in 1994, made a decisive move away from traditional arts policy towards a more inclusive approach that included film and television, while reframing the Australian creative industries in economic as well as cultural terms (Hawkins, 2014).

This set the stage, three years later, for the 1997 UK Labour Government to embrace a creative industries approach. In a symbolic shift from the old to the new, they replaced the Department of National Heritage (1992–1997) with the Department of Culture, Media and Sport (DCMS). Under the leadership of Chris Smith, the DCMS became emblematic of the new economic landscape of innovation and creativity, technology and the fast-globalising media industries (Hesmondhalgh et al., 2015). This was the age of 'Cool Britannia' when the creative industries were seen as shaping and defining British culture and identity while boosting the UK economy.

John Howkins' (2002) book on *The Creative Economy* and Richard Florida's (2002) essay on the importance of 'the creative class' – as drivers of innovation and economic growth in a digital world – placed the creative industries and creative occupations more generally – at the heart of 21st-century economies. They argued that creativity was a key driver of prosperity in a world where assets are increasingly bound up with intellectual rather than physical property – in ideas rather than objects (the 'intangible economy'). The creative industries were not only growing faster than other sectors, they were also central to the development of the economy as a whole. The creative economy, in other words, included the creative industries but went beyond them, incorporating creative workers – such as designers and content creators – in most industrial sectors.

The identification – and celebration – of the creative industries as economic drivers coincided with the decline of manufacturing across much of the developed world. Urban areas keen to regenerate – both through a start-up culture and attracting inward investment – embraced the idea of the 'creative city'. Creative cities were imagined as places that sparked innovation and economic growth, as well as being seen as more dynamic and more attractive places to live. Jason Potts and Stuart Cunningham (2008) described this policy shift: "In the past," they wrote,

> policymakers have treated creative industries as a welfare sector or as a sector that has no particular effects on other economic sectors. Evidence now suggests that creative industries may be considered economic growth drivers or, indeed, that they may play an even more strategic role in the innovation system as catalysts of variety creation and facilitators of systemic evolution.
>
> (p.10)

In 2013 Nesta published their *Manifesto for the Creative Economy*, making a powerful case for putting the cultural and creative at the heart of government policy (Bakhshi et al., 2013). In the same year, the UK Government, through the DCMS, developed a methodology for identifying the creative industries to capture and measure their economic impact[1] – marking a moment when the creative industries came into being as an identifiable economic category in the UK. The size, scale and growth trajectory of the creative industries was now a demonstrably significant part of the UK (and global) economy: a point made with increasing force by bodies like Nesta, the Creative Industries Council and the Creative Industries Federation in the UK.

In 2017 the UK Government, under pressure to include the creative industries in its industrial strategy, commissioned an *Independent Review of the Creative Industries*. Peter Bazelgette's report was unequivocal, positioning the creative industries at the heart of the UK's rapidly growing digital economy: a sector that was not only a UK success in its own right but with a range of positive interventions across the economy as a whole. One of its strongest recommendations was to support regional creative industries clusters across the UK, with a focus on innovation, intellectual property (IP) and talent development (Bazalgette, 2017). The government responded by funding the Creative Industries Clusters Programme (CICP), which supported, with industrial strategy funding (through the AHRC), the establishment of nine creative industries clusters across the UK. This move could be seen as a standard part of an industrial strategy, investing in innovation to promote sectorial economic dynamism and growth. But there was a crucial difference. This was the first time the creative industries had been included in a significant Research, Development and Innovation (R,D&I) programme. Following the CICP programme (Lewis et al., 2023) we could see further large-scale investments by governments – led by different political parties – across the four nations of the UK and beyond.

The character, critical landscape and value of the creative industries

The CICP initiative – creating a series of creative industries clusters across the UK, with a remit to use research and development (R&D) to develop new products, services and experiences – was a kind of R,D&I project in its own right. The nine clusters were tasked with introducing R&D (to a sector traditionally excluded from such practices) as a way to boost creative innovation. In so doing, they were addressing a fundamental question: **what is R,D&I in the creative industries?** This book is an attempt to answer this question. Before we do so, however, it is important to sketch out the critical landscape.

The rise of the creative economy in policy terms has been accompanied by an academic backlash against what many see as an uncritical embrace of the creative industries as *no more than* another economic sector. Philip Schlesinger (2017) argues that while the notion of the creative economy has been important politically, it comes at a price: a policy realm where culture is secondary, invariably trumped by the logic of economics. Perhaps the best metaphor for this reductionist way of thinking was articulated by Ronald Reagan's Federal Communications Commission's commissioner Mark Fowler (who oversaw widespread deregulation of the media and communications industries in the US): he described television as no more than a 'toaster with pictures'.

In this critique, cultural values – on people's experiences, identities and well-being – are subsidiary. Any subsidies to support local or distinctive cultures – from film to folk music – could be ruled as a restraint on global, free market competition. Justin O'Connor's 2023 book, *Culture is not an industry*, develops this critique of the 'economic turn' in the creative industries, arguing for a reassertion of cultural values. The uncritical embrace of the 'creative class' as a positive force in economic regeneration has also come under critical scrutiny. The growth of creative cities and the intangible economy has done little to address – and arguably exacerbated – a growth in inequality (Pratt, 2008; Haskel & Westlake, 2017). The creative industries have become hugely dependent on freelance labour, in many ways defining the rise of the precarious 'gig economy'. While equality and inclusion were always a problem for the traditional arts, this has become true for the creative industries more generally, made worse by a series of employment practices (word of mouth, low pay and long hours at entry level) that limit both access to employment and job security.

This leaves us at an interesting moment when prodigious growth alongside a number of research-led policy initiatives have made the creative industries a compelling proposition for policymakers, while its form and structure have become increasingly subject to critical examination in the academy. Part of the problem – implicit in some of the critical literature – is that the 'economic turn' in the creative industries has been associated with a neo-liberal orthodoxy (see, for example, Leger, 2011), where the purpose of public investment is to drive private profit.

There is a slippage here, where neo-liberal economics is conflated with economics as a whole. While this is understandable in a political context where neo-liberalism has been a dominant force, it is also reductive. To paraphrase: many other economic approaches are available – from neo-Keynesian to a focus on the foundational economy[2] – where economic strategies can be used to promote social, cultural and environmental outcomes. So, for example, investing in strong public service media backed by public-interest regulation produces different cultural and democratic outcomes than countries relying on market forces (Curran et al., 2013).

In this book, we want to move outside these confines. Rather than rejecting the economic turn, we argue that we need to rethink it. Wherever it lies on the complex spectrum between the subsidised arts or the commercial creative industries, most cultural activity needs to be paid for: preferably in ways that are equitable and sustainable. We need economic systems and structures that favour creative activities that provide positive social and cultural outcomes. We also need to acknowledge the importance of both economic and cultural values (Komorowski et al., 2021b). This also means addressing the many ways in which economic conditions shape – or constrain – culture and creativity. If we want a more inclusive, greener creative economy – one that celebrates a diversity of voices, limits environmental damage (Lupu et al., 2023) and generates a strong local tax base for funding public services – we need to develop the economic strategies and systems best able to deliver them.

This is a space where critical scrutiny can inform – rather than run counter to – policy development, based on an understanding of the creative industries that takes account of its history and its complexities (Komorowski & Lewis, 2023). Its size and significance matter, but so does its ability to work for the people it employs, for its audiences and for our broader cultural environment. Economics is inescapable: any cultural strategy must be underpinned by economic conditions that make it possible.

Despite significant advances, the data picture of the creative industries remains incomplete, for three main reasons. First, because of its dependence on a large freelance workforce, who are excluded from most UK data sets, it is difficult to make accurate estimates of the size of the creative industries. Second, while we have information about the scale of the creative industries (excluding freelancers), we know much less about the size and shape of the embedded creative workforce (creative workers working outside the creative sector). Third, the delineation of the creative industries is neither absolute nor fixed – what is a 'creative industry and what is not?' This is made more complex by the different classifications of the creative industries. UNESCO (Times, Cultural, 2015) establishes six cultural domains: heritage, performance, visual arts and crafts, books and press, audio-visual and interactive media, design and creative services. UNCTAD,[3] on the other hand, defines four domains: heritage, arts, media and functional creations. A more encompassing definition is provided by the UK Government's DCMS: 'Those industries which have their origin in individual creativity, skill and talent and which have a potential for wealth and job creation through the generation and exploitation of intellectual property.' This definition includes the following sectors: Advertising and marketing, Architecture, Design and designer fashion, Film, TV, video and radio, IT, software and computer services, Publishing and Music, performing and visual arts.[4] Creative companies can be either capital intensive or knowledge intensive. In both cases the symbolic and intangible nature of their products is what characterises these companies as creative and cultural (Peris-Ortiz et al., 2019).

To enable data creation and because of its widespread use, we have chosen to adopt the DCMS's definition of the creative industries. This is not without its flaws (so, for example, we might question the inclusion of some parts of the technology sector, as well as the exclusion of a number of creative activities from hospitality to hairdressing), but it allows us to make comparisons with existing UK data sets. The DCMS definition of the creative economy also includes people in creative occupations outside the creative industries (embedded creatives in other sectors, like designers or content creators). So, while the creative industries are a focal point, they are a subset of a larger creative economy, in a world where communication and creative content are an ubiquitous part of work and leisure.

What we do know from these data is that the economic importance of the creative industries in the UK (as in many other parts of the world) is substantial and growing. The latest estimate – at the time of writing – published by the DCMS[5] shows that in 2022 DCMS sectors contributed £169.4 billion to the UK economy. This was 7.7% of the total UK GVA. Creative Industries GVA grew faster than the UK economy both from 2021 to 2022 (9.8% vs 4.4%), and in the longer term from 2010 to 2022 (50.3% vs 21.5%).

The data we have gathered for this book is based on Wales, one of the four devolved nations of the UK. Wales is not untypical of many European nations and regions. As one of the world's first industrial nations, its history is bound up with mining and manufacturing, industries which have been in steady decline since the 1970s. Like many post-industrial places, the creative industries have become increasingly important to the Welsh economy, particularly in the Cardiff Capital Region (CCR) – the ten local authorities around Cardiff (Komorowski et al., 2021a). The creative industries are seen as a priority sector for economic development by both the Welsh Government and regional and local authorities.

While the creative industries are clustered throughout Wales, they are concentrated in and around Cardiff, the Welsh capital and across South Wales.[6] Estimates for 2022 show that there are approximately 10,500 enterprises active in the creative industries in Wales (Fodor et al., 2023). Over the last decade, Wales has seen particular growth in the film and TV sectors: South Wales now has more TV studios than anywhere in the UK outside London, and Cardiff is the UK's third largest film and TV industry employer after London and Manchester (Fodor et al., 2024).

In recent years, the Welsh film and TV sector has produced a range of global titles in high-end TV drama – such as *Dr Who* (BBC/Disney), *Sherlock* (BBC), *His Dark Materials* (HBO/BBC), *Sex Education* (Netflix). It has seen the rise of 'Welsh noir' TV series like *Hinterland* and *Hidden*.[7] It has provided a range of continuing series for UK broadcasters (such as *Casualty*, *Songs of Praise* and *Only Connect*) and is home to one of Europe's largest minority language broadcasters (S4C), making it the UK's centre for bilingual production. But, like many European small nations or regions, it risks being a 'show and go' production centre, providing landscapes, backdrops and a skilled workforce but developing or keeping little of the IP associated with these titles.

More generally, the success of the creative industries in Wales is fragile: 96% of creative businesses in Wales are small (very close to the UK average) (Komorowski et al., 2021b), supported by a large freelance workforce. They have a strong desire but little capacity to innovate. They lack the time and resources enjoyed by global media and digital companies – many of which are US based – to do R&D or to exploit their IP across genres.

Introduction to Clwstwr: Creative industries R,D&I in Wales

Creating Clwstwr

The CICP, we have suggested, represents a key moment in UK policy, as one of the UK's first comprehensive attempts to support R,D&I in the creative industries. It was an experimental initiative, designed to support a range of creative industries clusters across the UK, funded from the UK Government's industrial strategy through the AHRC.[8] The £120 million investment awarded nine R&D partnerships based around clusters in the UK and was meant to 'drive innovation and growth across the UK's creative industries, to encourage a new type of applied research'. The process of choosing the UK clusters was highly competitive, with 65 regions of the UK putting in bids during a year-long process, whittled down to an initial shortlist of 22 and a final list of 12, from which 9 successful clusters were selected (in Belfast, Bristol, Cardiff, Dundee, Edinburgh, Leeds, York and two in London).[9]

Clwstwr[10] (Welsh for cluster), the successful bid from Wales, focused on the audio-visual sector – already strong in Wales – but was keen to engage with a wide range of creative sectors whose work incorporated screen technologies or news and public information. Clwstwr was led by Cardiff University (by the team that set up Creative Cardiff, a 4,000-member network of creatives in South Wales[11]), in partnership with Cardiff Metropolitan University and the University of South Wales (USW) – all of whom provided in-kind support. Clwstwr received £5.3 million in funding from the CICP programme, with additional funding of £2.6 million from the Welsh Government and support in-kind from BBC Cymru Wales, the Arts Council of Wales and Cardiff Council, whose Head of Innovation (BBC), Head of Digital (Arts Council) and Culture Lead (Cardiff Council) formed part of Clwstwr's Management Team, alongside leads from the three universities.

This was the first initiative of its kind in Wales, and indeed, the first time the three universities had worked together in this way. Each university has complementary strengths in creative industries training, research and engagement including centres of excellence such as Cardiff University's School of Journalism, Media and Culture, the substantial creative industries training programmes at the USW and Cardiff Metropolitan University's PDR, an international centre for user-centred design-driven R&D.

The Clwstwr programme was designed to provide small, independent companies with the time, resources and support for R&D, and to embed innovation in the Welsh media sector. Its goals were economic, social and cultural – values built into its assessment criteria. It was, in this sense, developing an alternative economic strategy, a step towards levelling the playing field with global, highly integrated media companies with R,D&I budgets and built-in collaborations for IP development. It embraced a quadruple helix model of innovation (Steenkamp, 2019): curating interactions and engagement between academia, industry, government and civil society; working with a range of stakeholders in the cluster and identifying the relationships and value flows between them. Its goals were economic, social and cultural:

- To create an ecosystem that provided a network of independent companies and freelancers with the capacity to innovate and develop new IP, enhancing economic sustainability and growth, thereby increasing the local tax base (in ways that enticing US corporates to make content in Wales does not);
- To encourage socially useful and environmentally sustainable innovation, while promoting diversity and inclusion;
- To enhance the capacity of communities in Wales to tell their own stories, in both Welsh and English.

During the bid development stage, the Clwstwr team spoke to over 100 creative companies and freelancers about the potential of R,D&I to create new products, new ways of working, new services and new experiences. Some – usually SMEs in more technically focused areas like post-production – were aware of the potential of R&D. But for most, innovation methodologies were mysterious or elusive. R&D was seen as another country: usually, a patriarchy populated by men in white coats, with its own esoteric practices and language. The team were, as a consequence, aware that introducing the creative industries to the world of R,D&I – while simultaneously rethinking it – would be a key challenge.

Clwstwr's strategy was to deliver a two-way process of culture change. This meant working with the sector to explain and reimagine R,D&I: what it was and how it might help them develop new ideas. The broad aim was to foster a culture of R,D&I in a sector where the primary focus is often moving from one job/commission to the next. This was a process of exploration, redefining R,D&I processes for people working in the creative industries. So, for example, it meant challenging the widespread assumption – both within and outside creative industries – that R,D&I was necessarily about *technological* innovation: but it might involve innovations in forms of storytelling or new, more effective ways of working. Clwstwr's approach throughout was iterative, involving experimentation, regular reviews and reappraisals.

At the heart of the Clwstwr programme was an *innovation funding pipeline*, designed to provide training, guidance and funding to support company-led R,D&I. It was structured around an innovation ecosystem: a system of 'wraparound support' in R&D methodologies, research and commercialisation. This would sit alongside a range of *community building, networking* and *outreach* activities, designed to foster a culture of systemic innovation while promoting R,D&I to creatives from a wide range of backgrounds.

Clwstwr's innovation pipeline

The innovation pipeline – which provided training and funding – was designed to allow multiple points of access and engagement for creative companies and freelancers, regardless of levels of experience and understanding of R,D&I. This was *not* an innovation funnel – in which the most innovative companies were funded and others weeded out – but a process that attempted to move *all* companies towards R&D-led innovation.

Clwstwr's R&D activity was driven by a team of R,D&I producers, with industry rather than academic backgrounds, who would connect creatives with researchers and other forms of expertise, working alongside the companies and freelancers as they undertook their R,D&I projects. Producer involvement began at an early stage, offering advice and support to companies to ensure their funding applications were in scope, with a clear R&D focus and the potential to create a new and sustainable product, process or experience.

The Clwstwr team chose user-centred design (UCD) as their principal R&D methodology, with training provided by UCD specialists based at PDR at Cardiff Metropolitan.[12] Ideas Labs were offered at the beginning of each funding round: these were designed to introduce smaller creative companies and freelancers to the concept and practice of R,D&I, so that they might be in a position to apply for funding. The Labs provided an opportunity to explore, develop and refine new ideas with the support of the PDR/Cardiff Metropolitan team, taking participants through a user-design process.

Clwstwr's initial approach was to offer a short, one-day Ideas Lab open to anyone on a first-come, first-served basis. While some members of this first cohort went on to develop successful innovations, the group lacked diversity – especially in terms of gender (over 90% of participants were male). This led to two immediate shifts in Clwstwr's approach:

- To move away from the traditional, technological language used around R&D, towards an emphasis on ideas rather than technologies, realised by various forms of innovation. This meant a focus on the conceptual core of R&D – the generation and systematic use of new knowledge as a pathway to innovation – rather than (simply) enabling technologies. So, for example, on its FAQ page, Clwstwr defined R&D as activities that were not 'business as usual', were novel (aimed at new findings), creative (based on original, not obvious concepts and hypotheses) and systematic (based on a planned and budgeted approach), with a level of uncertainty about the final outcomes;
- A recognition that developing an understanding of UCD required more time (a minimum of two days), and that, for many small companies and freelancers, this meant a loss of income. Henceforth, attendees for Ideas Labs received a stipend of £500 on completion, with childcare support available to support and enable their participation. The increase in demand that followed this change meant introducing a light-touch application process for Ideas Labs – which became the first stage of an annual training/funding cycle.

The Ideas Labs played a key role in developing R,D&I skills, while significantly broadening the pool of applicants to the funding rounds that followed. As these attendees put it:

> 'Clwstwr Ideas Lab has been brilliant in terms of supporting us as individuals to develop our research strategy. We're actually thinking about the opportunities and gaps in the market, and how our research could lead to a possible solution for that. It's been fun, thought-provoking and challenging as well. It is a fantastic opportunity for us as freelancers to really nurture our artistic practice and our ideas.' 'The lab has been great. It's really needed – its thinking about funding in a different kind of way and thinking about products in a different way.'

The first funding round – a £10,000 Seed Fund, for the development of early-stage R&D projects – was launched after the completion of Ideas Labs and was open to both participants and non-participants. Later in the year, at a time when Seed funding applicants would have been able to complete their projects, Clwstwr launched their Development Fund – up to £50,000 to support R&D projects with the potential for the development of economically sustainable new products, services or experiences. This was, again, open to both Seed funded and new applicants and was often the stage at which more 'R&D-ready' companies engaged with Clwstwr. The sequencing of these different tiers of training and funding made it possible (if challenging) for a small company or freelancer – for whom R,D&I was an entirely new concept – to go through all stages of the pipeline. Indeed, a small cohort in every one of the three funding rounds achieved this.

The Clwstwr innovation pipeline designed and delivered 9 funding calls over a 3-year period – with a total of £3.42 million of direct investment between 2019 and 2022 – funding a total of 85 lead companies across 118 projects from a pool of 550 applications. The largest category of funded companies and freelancers came from film, television, games and other audio-visual sectors, developing new forms and formats for storytelling across a range of genres (from news and documentary to podcasts to interactive film); adapting digital technologies to create new products (such as immersive technology to manage pain-relief, AI technologies to enhance journalism or geolocation to create new forms of media-based tourism); or using innovation to adapt and enhance production processes (from virtual set-building to remote editing). Clwstwr also supported screen or news-based innovations from a wide range of creative fields, including dance, journalism, music, theatre and the visual arts. Projects also spilt over into other parts of the economy and society, from healthcare to transport.

The 85 funded lead businesses collaborated with a wider innovation network in Wales: with more than 190 companies working on R&D

projects (including 273 individual freelancers hired to conduct R&D) and a total of more than 700 team members and freelancers. Two-thirds of the 118 funded projects were collaborative projects, where the lead businesses collaborated with at least one other business or freelancer.[13]

Clwstwr's R&D projects took an average of seven months to complete and focused on one of three main themes: creating new ways of working to build sustainable business models; engaging audiences and markets in new ways; and exploring new forms of storytelling. Many of these innovations – especially in areas like storytelling – were about cultural forms rather than technologies. Any new IP developed remained with the company leading the project.

The programme also aimed to address social and cultural challenges facing the region, promoting diversity, inclusivity, environmental sustainability and community engagement. The evaluation of project applications was therefore based on both their potential economic impact and the need for a positive social, cultural or environmental impact (both being equally weighted in the scoring criteria for funding applications). As Clwstwr evolved, thematic sessions were introduced around commercialisation, IP exploitation and protection and wider business support with experts Landsker, Upstarter and a commercial/IP lawyer (Angharad Evans). A series of knowledge-sharing and training events were also developed on key Clwstwr themes such as environmental sustainability and equality, diversity and inclusion.

Community building through Clwstwr

Clwstwr, like all the CICP programmes, was based on the principle that the creative industries need to engage in R&D to expand their sources of cultural, commercial and public value – while acknowledging that the language and practice of R&D is new territory to many in the creative industries. The unfamiliarity of R&D for many in the creative industries put communications and engagement at the heart of Clwstwr's activities. The challenge was to convert multiple audiences from varying levels of R,D&I understanding (many of the target audience having little to none) to actively engaging with systemic R,D&I processes. Clwstwr used a range of activities – including showcasing best practices, using new, jargon-free ways to communicate the benefits of R&D, and sharing expertise, guidance and learning – to change perceptions and encourage ambition. The Clwstwr communications strategy aimed to:

- Increase R&D activity resulting in new products, services and experiences;
- Raise awareness and engagement with innovation – from a diversity of groups – in the cluster;

- Promote economic and cultural growth for the region, and;
- Amplify Wales's international profile.

Clwstwr produced targeted messaging – with a focus on accessible content – through social media accounts, monthly e-newsletters, online resources and a mobile-responsive website featuring programme information, news and events, blogs, relevant research, project profiles and online log-in and application forms. Overall, Clwstwr's communications activity generated: a website with 306,008 page views (233,506 unique page views) and 73,679 unique users; 2,351 Twitter followers, 214 Facebook followers, 568 LinkedIn followers and 813 Instagram followers; 40 editions of the e-newsletter with 593 e-newsletter subscribers.

Real-time/live engagement focused on a series of 52 events across the programme – including both public-facing events and cohort-only sessions focusing on skills development, networking, knowledge transfer and the promotion of R&D projects, engaging more than 1,300 attendees in total. The R,D&I Producer team encouraged and broadened engagement with traditionally under-represented populations, hosting Clwstwr events, presenting at sector events and conducting over 1,000 1-2-1 meetings. These meetings were particularly useful in supporting the development of R&D ideas and subsequent bids to the Seed and Development funds. They also played a key role in connecting projects with a range of expertise, including UCD R&D processes, business development, commercialisation and academic expertise.

Clwstwr also provided a platform for creative businesses and freelancers in Wales (and beyond) to network to enable new connections and partnerships. The programme's events and knowledge-sharing initiatives fostered a strong sense of community among Clwstwr participants – particularly around certain areas or themes (so, for example, the cluster of projects around news and democracy became an informal collaborative network). Clwstwr's communications activities also raised the profile of the creative industries in Wales, positioning the region as a hub for innovation and creativity by presenting at industry events and conferences across the UK and internationally. So, for example, the Clwstwr team developed partnerships with other European creative cluster organisations like Media City Bergen and led a Welsh delegation to Los Angeles to meet with US-based studios and innovators.

ClwstwrVerse, Clwstwr's largest event, was the culmination of the Clwstwr programme. Held across two venues in July 2022, the two-day event showcased Welsh media innovation, celebrating the Clwstwr R,D&I projects. It was attended by 580 people – including investors and leaders of five European creative clusters – and featured a showcase space, talks, demos, experiences and experiments as well as investor sessions, panels and workshops. The value of this showcasing event for raising the profile of the cluster was expressed by an attendee, the innovation lead at NBC Universal:

> The thing that stood out to me about ClwstwrVerse was that the innovation happening in Cardiff was just mind-blowing. Everything that we're looking at as a studio, Universal Pictures, is completely relevant to what is happening in Cardiff. From augmented reality, virtual reality to virtual production and artificial intelligence, everything is happening in Cardiff.

This activity fed into the programme's broader aims – to increase the creative industries' propensity and capacity for innovation – while underpinning the success of each funding round by generating a wide range of strong applications from a diverse pool of companies and freelancers.

The need for a new understanding of R,D&I in the creative industries

Since R,D&I is widely acknowledged as a tool for economic growth, it has become part of European, national and regional policy agendas and the target for funding mechanisms (Nauwelaers & Wintjes, 2003). As we described earlier, the UK Government (and devolved Governments in Scotland, Wales and Northern Ireland) now includes the creative industries in its industrial strategy, making the case for public investment in creative industries R,D&I (Mateos-Garcia & Bakhshi, 2016). R,D&I has become increasingly important in the creative industries, both for policy makers and for the creative industries businesses themselves. So, for example, Bakhshi et al. (2010) highlight the need for arts and cultural organisations to engage in R&D in order to 'expand the sources of cultural, commercial and public value'. They explain how, in the context of rapid social, cultural and technical changes, the creative industries need to adapt, applying the systematic use of knowledge to shape the way they engage with society.

This has raised a number of new questions for the creative industries and policy makers: how do sectors accustomed to being a separate cultural domain, excluded from industrial strategies, respond to their sudden inclusion? Does government investment in R,D&I – its principal methods for stimulating increases in productivity, impact or growth – work for cultural and creative sectors, and if so, how? Can economic goals be delivered alongside social and cultural value? And do we need new approaches to R,D&I, which has, hitherto, been developed in fields like manufacturing, engineering, science and technology? Answers to these questions remain elusive, for a number of reasons:

1 The creative industries are still not fully integrated into R,D&I policy mechanisms. Despite the incorporation of the creative industries in policy development, many traditional ways of thinking about culture and the economy remain in place. At all levels of government, the creative industries often remain compartmentalised under 'culture' rather than 'the economy' – or else in a confusing mishmash between the two. In a world where success is often measured by hard economic metrics, this makes politicians and policy makers less inclined to take it seriously than more traditional economic sectors. Culture is, in many political circles, still seen as softer and less tangible, somehow less connected to economic policy staples like productivity and job creation. And while Arts Councils have broadened their reach, many of the main beneficiaries of government subsidies remain firmly in the realm of the traditional arts. We need to understand the creative industries as part of a mixed economy. It includes sectors that receive subsidies – in return for perceived cultural, social or economic benefits – and the more commercial industries. As a consequence, we would argue that the creative industries should be seen as a continuum rather than a simple binary: many arts organisations depend on public funding but still raise commercial revenue, while more commercial sectors, like film and TV production, often receive significant public subsidies through mechanisms like tax credits. The interplay between commercial and subsided activity – reflecting the mix of cultural, social and economic value generated – is complex. It cannot easily be grafted onto sub-sectors, while the benefits of subsidy can spread across sectors (support for theatre, for example, provides a talent pipeline for sectors like film and television).
2 The focus on quantifiable outputs and measurable R&D activities in existing R,D&I policy mechanisms often overlook the creative processes, social impact and cultural value generation that are central to innovation in the creative industries (Gustafsson & Lazzaro, 2021). While economic growth (also driven by creative industries innovation) has measurable indicators, it is much more difficult to quantify cultural and social values (Komorowski et al., 2023).
3 The creative industries have characteristics that make it difficult to put traditional R,D&I frameworks into practice. Creative enterprises, often small and financially precarious, face significant challenges in making adequate independent investments in R&D (Oakley, 2006).

The inherent nature of project-based creative employment contributes to this uncertainty by restricting the opportunity for long-term investment and generating unpredictable revenue streams. This creates an environment where R&D activities are rarely planned into the daily activities of creative industries businesses and organisations.

4 Assumptions about technology are present across policy domains in ways that can exclude the creative industries. This means that some countries, like the UK, require R&D to be connected to scientific or technological delivery to be eligible for tax credits, overtly stating that work rooted in the arts and humanities is not eligible for R&D tax claims (a position contradicted by its industrial strategy). The OECD's definition of high-tech sectors is also STEM oriented, including, for example, pharmaceuticals, the electronic industry, vehicle construction, the aerospace construction industry and engineering (Galindo-Rueda & Verger, 2016). While countries like Italy, France, Denmark, Spain and Norway take a broader view, including Social Sciences and Humanities within R&D tax credit programmes, innovation policies are often tailored towards so-called 'high-tech' sectors (Hirsch-Kreinsen, 2008). It follows that most studies of R,D&I have focused on scientific disciplines such as pharmacology, economics/management, mathematics, health, engineering, technology or applied sciences and are rarely connected to the domains of arts, culture and the creative industries (Bakhshi et al., 2013). The systemic tools behind industrial strategies – notably R,D&I – have been developed in relation to science, technology, manufacturing and mathematics (STEM), rather than in the social sciences, arts or humanities. This has led to techno-centric assumptions around R,D&I that often do not work for the creative industries.

5 R,D&I tends to be associated with a corporate business landscape, one in which governments work with big companies to boost pre-existing R&D capacity. As a consequence, both the concept and practice of R,D&I are new to the creative industries. Most regional creative clusters (Komorowski & Picone, 2020) do not fit the STEM model of corporate partnership, being made up of hundreds of small companies (routinely employing ten people or less) and a handful of larger SMEs (Komorowski & Lewis, 2021), with little or no expertise in (or resources devoted to) R,D&I.

6 Current forms of language around R,D&I support and processes are often a barrier for the creative industries. For example, the *Frascati Manual* relies on language rooted in scientific and technical contexts derived from STEM skill sets and related product markets (OECD, 2015). When Lomas (2017) analysed how the *Frascati Manual* might be applied to arts and culture, she found that various terms used in the innovation survey by the OECD and its studies are either not

understood or cannot be applied to innovation in arts and culture. While some creative sectors – such as theatre and performance – do use some of the terminology of R&D to describe their activity, most creative businesses are not familiar with its language and methodologies.

7 R,D&I in the creative industries can take various forms and create other kinds of (cultural) value, which tends to differentiate from R,D&I in other sectors. Innovation in the creative industries includes aesthetic innovation, cultural reinterpretation and creative expression (Snowball et al., 2022). Innovation in the creative industries is also bound up with the emergence of new business models, the ubiquitous presence of digitalisation and the intangible and increasingly cross-sector and public-interest nature of creative products. The collaborative nature of innovation is also part of innovation in the creative industries (Gustafsson & Lazzaro, 2021).

8 Finally, the current understanding of R&D tends to overemphasise a linear conception of novelty, when creative industries often thrive on more iterative processes where creators refine and adapt their work based on feedback, trends and evolving cultural contexts. This iterative approach, fundamental to creative practices (Wölbling et al., 2012), needs to be incorporated within R&D frameworks in the creative industries.

In the chapters that follow, we discuss in more detail existing frameworks, concepts and approaches to R,D&I and outline – based on our findings – how we should reframe R,D&I for the creative industries to support future research, policy making and creative industries practices.

Data insights of this book – Methodology

This book is informed by:

- Monitoring data collected from 118 R,D&I projects curated and funded by Clwstwr with 85 different creative industries partners, including interim and final reports;
- Case studies of selected projects;
- Over 500 survey responses from Clwstwr-funded and non-Clwstwr-funded businesses before and after Clwstwr's R,D&I intervention.

The methodology used to gather and analyse these data sets is outlined in more detail in Lewis et al. (2023). The primary data set for this book is based on extensive interviews from the 85 businesses funded by Clwstwr (for more details on projects and interviewees please see the Appendices). Each of the following chapters uses a specific analysis of these data (details of which can be found at the beginning of the Findings section of each chapter). Between November 2021 and January 2023, a total of 68 interviews were conducted with businesses and sole traders participating in R&D through the Clwstwr programme. Several businesses went through multiple funding rounds, so the 68 interviews covered a total of 91 R&D projects. Each interview session lasted between one and two hours and followed a customised framework rooted in cultural theory and value creation processes.

The methodology drew upon the conceptual framework established by Fuller et al. (2011), which scrutinises the emergence of value within the cultural and creative industries. This model was modified to align with the Clwstwr programme, taking into account three of its focal areas: environmental sustainability, Equality, Diversity and Inclusion (EDI) and R&D leadership. The resulting model shaped the interview structure and facilitated the comprehensive collection of R&D data across Fuller et al.'s three levels of value generation (2011) – reflexivity, operability and sensitivity. The methodological framework led to the design of a two-step interview process. The first phase aimed to explore the value and impact of R&D using an experimental lens that made use of phenomenological approaches and graphic elicitation tools (Copeland & Agosto, 2012). The second part explored, in more depth, the impact and value of R&D through a series of targeted questions.

The first part of the interview made use of the Miro platform to collect qualitative data. Interviewees were asked to draw a line on a graph to represent their own R&D experience, which was assessed against both the project timeline and their level of expectations. The drawing process was accompanied by a verbal explanation of the undertaken R&D journey, informing the indicators synthesised by the graph. After illustrating their R&D experience, participants were asked to select from a series of ten key performance indicators (KPIs), which they believed applied to their own projects, i.e. areas where the impact was tangible. Interviewees could choose from the following KPIs: R&D effectiveness (e.g. novelty, time), Clwstwr support (e.g. interaction with support staff, participation in training, workshops and participation in events), developed IP (e.g. patents and copyright), new business opportunities, widening audience base, environmental/social/cultural value, new staff, local and international partnerships/networks and business growth opportunities (e.g. productivity, exports, turnover and R&D tax claims).

For the analysis in Chapters 2 and 3 we coded graph narratives using Nvivo software, following an inductive reasoning approach (see respective chapters for more details). For the quantitative analysis in Chapter 4 we have encoded all drawings recording the R&D journeys of Clwstwr projects following uniform criteria and applied statistical methods (see Chapter 4 for more details). The second part of the interview focused on specific questions to explore the impact of R&D on their businesses. These covered:

- R&D (novelty of R&D processes, time invested in R&D, changing understanding of R&D);
- The application process (description of the process, support during application, challenges in applying, user-friendliness);
- Clwstwr support (most beneficial support, additional support);
- Developed IP (planned and reached TRL level, registered IP, importance of IP, approach to open innovation);
- Business growth (spin-offs, expansion possibilities, turnover growth, staff growth, staff upskilling);
- Audience growth (new audiences reached, learnings);
- Approaches to sustainability (values, learnings, communication of values, targeted sustainable development goals);
- Partnerships (closed local partnerships, closed international partnerships), and;
- Future outlook (major challenges in the next five years).

While all the questions contributed to a qualitative data set, some provided quantifiable data. We used a grounded approach for the qualitative data analysis to establish the most impactful aspects for businesses in terms of R,D&I. The responses provided in the second part informed research results across the chapters. For example, in Chapter 3 we combined the Nvivo analysis with the responses from specific questions addressed in the second part of the interview to determine the number of innovators falling into specific typologies. To assign learning scores, we used the questions falling under the 'growth' KPI area, where respondents were asked to assess the impact of their project on learning and new staff. For the R&D focus score, we coded questions falling under the R&D KPI area, where respondents were asked to assess the nature of their R&D processes within their projects.

This mixed-methods approach informs our findings and discussions throughout the book. More details about the methodologies and analysis applied can be found throughout the following chapters. The main purpose of the book is to reframe the concept and processes of R&D in this sector, moving beyond old R,D&I paradigms borrowed from technical and scientific domains. In doing so, it builds on empirical data from the Clwstwr project, progressively organised into five chapters that introduce in turn the historical context of the development of R&D (Chapter 1), businesses' perception of R&D in the creative industries (Chapter 2), a novel framework for R&D-led typologies of innovation (Chapter 3), optimal levels of support for creative businesses conducting R&D (Chapter 4) and overarching conclusions and recommendations for building a thriving creative economy through the lens of R&D (Chapter 5).

Notes

1 Creative Industries Economic Estimates Methodology, DCMS: https://assets.publishing.service.gov.uk/government/uploads/system/uploads/attachment_data/file/499683/CIEE_Methodology.pdf.
2 See, for example, https://foundationaleconomy.com/.
3 UNCTAD Classifications: http://unctadstat.unctad.org/EN/Classifications.html.
4 https://assets.publishing.service.gov.uk/media/5a7c0b3de5274a7202e19327/Classifying_and_Measuring_the_Creative_Industries_Consultation_Paper_April_2013-final.pdf.
5 The full data can be found via https://www.gov.uk/government/statistics/dcms-and-digital-sector-gva-2022-provisional/dcms-sectors-economic-estimates-gross-value-added-2022-provisional.
6 A full data picture of the creative industries in Wales is available at https://maps.datahubclub.uk/atlas.
7 https://rts.org.uk/article/all-things-bleak-and-beautiful-rise-welsh-noir.
8 https://creativeindustriesclusters.com/.
9 https://culturecounts.scot/news/shortlist-announced-creative-industries-clusters-programme.
10 https://clwstwr.org.uk/.
11 https://creativecardiff.org.uk/.
12 https://www.cardiffmet.ac.uk/pdr/Pages/default.aspx.
13 A full list of funded projects is available at https://clwstwr.org.uk/projects.

References

Adorno, T., & Horkheimer, M. (1947). The culture industry. In *Dialectic of enlightenment*, translated by E. Jephcott. Stanford: Stanford University Press.

Bakhshi, H., Freeman, A., & Desai, R. (2010). *Not rocket science: A roadmap for arts and cultural R&D*. London: MissionModelsMoney. missionmodelsmoney.org.uk/sites/default/files/23974477-Not-Rocket-Science-Hasan-Bakhshi-et-al-2010_0.pdf

Bakhshi, H., Hargreaves, I., & Mateos-Garcia, J. (2013). A manifesto for the creative economy. https://media.nesta.org.uk/documents/a--manifesto-for-the-creative-economy-april13.pdf

Bazalgette, P. (2017). *Independent review of the creative industries*, UK Govt, https://www.gov.uk/government/publications/independent-review-of-the-creative-industries

Bourdieu, P. (2018). Distinction: A social critique of the judgement of taste. In D. Grusky (Ed.), *Inequality* (pp. 287–318). London: Routledge.

Copeland, A. J., & Agosto, D. E. (2012). Diagrams and relational maps: The use of graphic elicitation techniques with interviewing for data collection, analysis, and display. *International Journal of Qualitative Methods*, *11*(5), 513–533.

Curran, J. P., Soroka, S., Andrew, B., Aalberg, T., Iyengar, S., Coen, S., … & Tiffen, R. (2013). Auntie knows best? Public broadcasting and public affairs knowledge. *British Journal of Political Science*, *43*(4), 719–739. ISSN 0007-1234.

Florida, R. (2002). *The rise of the creative class: And how it's transforming work, leisure, community and everyday life*. New York: Basic Books.

Fodor, M. M., Komorowski, M. & Lewis, J. (2023). Clwstwr creative industries report no 1.3 – Report update: The size and composition of the creative industries in Wales in 2022 (Building resilience after COVID-19). Clwstwr publication series, Cardiff, Clwstwr. https://clwstwr.org.uk/sites/default/files/2023-09/Creative%20Industries%20Report%20No%201_3_Final.pdf

Fodor, M. M., Komorowski, M. & Lewis, J. (2024). *Industry insights: Cardiff capital region's media sector 2021*. Cardiff: Center for the Creative Economy. https://indd.adobe.com/view/2d5086d2-0669-403e-b024-9f8e1775ce3f ISBN 978-1-7394553-4-7.

Fuller, T., Warren, L., & Norman, S. J. (2011). Creative methodologies for understanding a creative industry. In C. Henry, & A. de Briun (Eds.), *Entrepreneurship and the Creative Economy*. Cheltenham: Edward Elgar Publishing.

Galindo-Rueda, F., & Verger, F. (2016). *OECD taxonomy of economic activities based on R&D intensity*. OECD. https://www.oecd-ilibrary.org/docserver/5jlv73sqqp8r-en.pdf?expires=1734037784&id=id&accname=guest&checksum=8518CD062BA32301F07DC52DAADDB5CC

Gustafsson, C., & Lazzaro, E. (2021). The innovative response of cultural and creative industries to major European societal challenges: Toward a knowledge and competence base. *Sustainability*, *13*(23), 13267.

Haskel, J. & Westlake, S. (2017), *Capitalism without capital: The rise of the intangible economy*, Princeton, New Jersey: Princeton University Press.

Hawkins, R. (2014). Paul Keating's creative nation: A policy document that changed us. *The Conversation*. https://theconversation.com/paul-keatings-creative-nation-a-policy-document-that-changed-us-33537

Hesmondhalgh, D., Oakley, K., Lee, D., & Nisbett, M. (2015). *Culture, economy and politics: The case of new labour*. London: Palgrave Macmillan.

Hirsch-Kreinsen, H. (2008). 'Low-technology': A forgotten sector in innovation policy. *Journal of Technology Management & Innovation*, *3*(3), 11–20.

Howkins, J. (2002). *The creative economy: How people make money from ideas*. London: Penguin UK.

Komorowski, M., Fodor, M., & Lewis, J. (2021a). Clwstwr creative industries report no. 2: The media sector in the Cardiff capital region. Project report. [Online]. Clwstwr. Available at: https://clwstwr.org.uk/clwstwr-creative-industries-report-no-2-media-sector-cardiff-capital-region-driving-economic-growth

Komorowski, M., Fodor, M., Lewis, J., & Pepper, S. (2023). Creative hubs and intercultural dialogue—towards a new socio-economic narrative.

Sustainability, *15*(10), article number: 8282. https://doi.org/10.3390/su15108282

Komorowski, M., & Lewis, J. (2021). Ckwstwr policy brief no 1: The (potential) impact of Brexit on creative businesses. Implications for policy and businesses in Wales. Cardiff: Available at: https://clwstwr.org.uk/sites/default/files/2020-07/Clwstwr%20Policy%20Brief%20No%201_FINAL.pdf

Komorowski, M., & Lewis, J. (2023). The creative and cultural industries: Towards sustainability and recovery. *Sustainability*, *15*(13), article number: 9923. https://doi.org/10.3390/su15139923

Komorowski, M., Lupu, R., Lewis, J., & Pepper, S. (2021b) Joining the dots—understanding the value generation of creative networks for sustainability in local creative ecosystems. *Sustainability*, *13*(22), article number: 12352. https://doi.org/10.3390/su132212352

Komorowski, M., & Picone, I. (Eds.). (2020). *Creative cluster development: Governance, place-making and entrepreneurship*. London: Routledge.

Leger, M. (Ed.). (2011). *Culture and contestation in the new century, intellect books*.

Lewis, J. (1990). *Art, culture and enterprise*. London: Routledge.

Lewis, J., Komorowski, M., Fodor, M., Lupu, R., Pepper, S., Walters, L., & McLeod, K. (2023). Clwstwr, A model for research, development and innovation in the creative industries. The Centre for the Creative Economy. https://clwstwr.org.uk/sites/default/files/2023-06/Clwstwr_A%20model%20for%20research%2C%20development%20and%20innovation%20in%20the%20creative%20industries_Web.pdf

Lomas, E. (2017). Defining R&D for the arts and knowledge cultural domains. UCL, Available at: https://discovery.ucl.ac.uk/id/eprint/1543295/1/R%26D_FinalReport_elomas_ahrc_ucl_2017.pdf

Lupu, R., Komorowski, M., Lewis, J., Mothersdale, G., & Pepper, S. (2023). Greening the audiovisual sector: Towards a new understanding through innovation practices in Wales and beyond. *Sustainability*, *15*(4), article number: 2975. https://doi.org/10.3390/su15042975

Mateos-Garcia, J., & Bakhshi, H. (2016). *The geography of creativity in the UK*. London: Nesta.

Nauwelaers, C. C. E. M. G., & Wintjes, R. J. M. (2003). Towards a new paradigm for innovation policy? In B. Asheim, A. Isaksen, C. Nauwelaers, & F. Totdling (Eds.), *Regional innovation policy for small-medium enterprises* (pp. 193–210). Cheltenham: Edward Elgar Publishing.

O'Connor, J. (2023). *Culture is not an industry: Reclaiming art and culture for the common good*. Manchester: Manchester University Press.

Oakley, K. (2006). Include us out—Economic development and social policy in the creative industries. *Cultural Trends*, *15*(4), 255–273.

OECD, Manual, Frascati. (2015). Guidelines for collecting and reporting data on research and experimental development. Available at: http://www.oecd.org/sti/frascati-manual-2015-9789264239012-en.htm

Peris-Ortiz, M., Gomez, J. A., & López-Sieben, M. (2019). Cultural and creative industries: An overview. *Cultural and Creative Industries: A Path to Entrepreneurship and Innovation*, 1–13.

Potts, J. (2009). Introduction: Creative industries & innovation policy. *Innovation*, *11*(2), 138–147.

Potts, J., & Cunningham, S. (2008). Four models of the creative industries. *International Journal of Cultural Policy*, *14*(3), 233–247.

Pratt, A. (2008). Creative cities: The cultural industries and the creative class. *Geografiska Annaler, Series B: Human Geography*, *90* (2), 107–117. ISSN 0435-3684.

Schlesinger, P. (2017). The creative economy invention of a global orthodoxy in innovation. *The European Journal of Social Science Research*, *1*, 30.

Snowball, J., Tarentaal, D., & Sapsed, J. (2022). Innovation and diversity in the digital cultural and creative industries. In J. Woronkowicz (Ed.), *Arts, entrepreneurship, and innovation* (pp. 187–215). Cham: Springer Nature Switzerland.

Steenkamp, R. J. (2019). The quadruple helix model of innovation for Industry 4.0. *Acta Commercii*, *19*(1), 1–10.

Wölbling, A., Krämer, K., Buss, C. N., Dribbisch, K., LoBue, P., & Taherivand, A. (2012). Design thinking: An innovative concept for developing user-centered software. In A. Maedche, A. Botzenhardt, & L. Neer (Eds.), *Software for people: Fundamentals, trends and best practices* (pp. 121–136). Berlin/Heidelberg: Springer Science & Business Media.

2 Rethinking R&D in the creative industries

Ruxandra Lupu

The importance of a sector-specific understanding of R&D

Research and Development (R&D) can be described as a process: the generation and systematic use of new knowledge, leading to innovation. Once done in dedicated laboratories by specialists and supported by large budgets, R&D has become a much more accessible and common practice. It has, over time, evolved from the traditional and linear model of creating innovation (Schumpeter, 1934) to an increasingly multi-faceted process. This has led to the adoption of R&D by different knowledge domains, including, more recently, the creative industries (see Chapter 1).

Despite the increased attention dedicated to R&D from a scientific, industry and policy perspective, the understanding of R&D processes inside the creative industries remains limited. We have only a vague idea about how creative businesses actually understand R&D – what value they attribute to it or how they define it. This limits creative businesses' practical experience in dealing with R&D and the mechanisms underpinning it. This is compounded by the way in which theoretical and practical understandings of the concept tend to be still fuelled by general definitions that use technocratic or STEM-focused language that is often inaccessible to creative businesses.

We need to review R&D processes in ways that come from – and work within – the creative industries, rather than simply transposing generalised or borrowed concepts and practices from other sectors. This chapter addresses the limits of how creative industries businesses understand R&D within their own sector. In doing so, it analyses businesses' perceptions about R&D in terms of value assigned to R&D processes and how these perceptions give rise to specific sector-relevant characteristics of R&D.

To explore these questions, we conducted interviews with 68 freelancers or businesses (from December 2021 – January 2023), funded and supported by Clwstwr to do R&D, as part of the UK's CICP (see Chapter 1). We used a mix of methods, combining quantitative and qualitative

DOI: 10.4324/9781003481805-2

This chapter has been made available under a CC BY-NC-ND 4.0 license.

approaches. The quantitative approach assessed three important values determining the perception of R&D for creative businesses: the value of novelty of R&D practices, the time-based value of such practices and go-to-market value. We used qualitative analysis to identify the characteristics that creative businesses assign to R&D within their sector: using inductive thematic analysis to first generate codes for R&D traits, before grouping them under a common theme or concept delimiting a concrete semantic area (see Chapter 1 for more methodological details).

We begin with a literature review of the context fuelling the limited knowledge around the understanding of R&D processes within the creative industries. The findings section then explores the value that creative businesses assign to R&D, before moving on to discuss how from these values emerge specific R&D characteristics. In the conclusion, we discuss how an empirical approach to the understanding of R&D within the creative industries can shape R&D practices and policies in the future.

Towards a practical understanding of R&D

There are two major limits to understanding R&D processes in the creative industries:

- The first emerges from the definitions of R&D that are largely recognised, adopted and circulated by governments and funding bodies and generally developed outside the creative industries.
- The second emerges from the complexity of R&D processes within the creative industries, which often do not operate in the terms and frameworks developed in STEM disciplines and sectors. This complexity also limits the number of available studies on R&D processes.

The most widely recognised and internationally adopted definition of R&D is provided by the *Frascati Manual* (OECD, 2015). Originally published in 1963, the definition has been adjusted over time to match the spread of R&D practices across different knowledge domains. The updated 2015 version of the definition acknowledged R&D as: ‘the creative and systematic work undertaken in order to increase the stock of knowledge – including knowledge of humankind, culture and society – and to devise new applications of available knowledge.’ It further differentiates between three different processes of R&D: basic research, applied research and experimental development. Basic research describes the acquisition of knowledge without any immediate application or use; applied research is directed towards a specific aim or objective; and experimental development works towards a very concrete output such as a product, service, experience or process.

Bakhshi and Lomas (2017) have criticised the *Frascati Manual*'s R&D definitions for not including all possible R&D processes – especially for the creative industries and the arts and cultural sectors. We would agree with this, but would argue that the problem for the creative industries lies less in these basic definitions – since the updated version of the *Frascati Manual* is inclusive of various R&D processes across sectors – but in the customs, practices and assumptions clustered around perceptions of – and policies towards – R&D. These customs and practices are still largely dominated and informed by examples from technology and science.

According to the *R&D in the Creative Industries Survey* (2020), a majority of responding creative businesses in the UK (55%) use the *Frascati* definition when implementing R&D, while a minority (14%) use a tax definition. Nearly a third – 31% – use neither the *Frascati* nor the tax claim definition, suggesting the need for a definition that better aligns with the nature of activities in the creative industries. The study points to a perception of R&D that is more related to investment in projects and content rather than in technologies and process/product innovation.

Bakhshi and Lomas (2017) also see the importance of R&D for the creative industries and shed light on the complexity of understanding R&D processes in these sectors. At present, R&D concepts are still used ambiguously (Bakhshi et al., 2021) and interchangeably with the notion of innovation. R&D represents instead *a potential pathway leading to innovation*, informed by practices like market research, training and design (Nesta, 2006). R&D can also take other forms that are more suitable to the specific ways in which creative industries generate and transfer knowledge. For example, market research that is experimental and methodologically sophisticated could be labelled as R&D (Bakhshi, 2022). Emerging organisational forms such as CreaTech businesses (Kaleniuk & Kuznetsova, 2022) can give rise to specific forms of conceptualising and implementing R&D (Siepel et al., 2022). These observations point to the importance of defining R&D both in terms of various processes and delivery models (sole traders, SMEs, collaborations/networks and large businesses).

While Bakhshi and Lomas (2017) consider the specificities of R&D across the creative industries, other recent studies tend to focus on specific, sub-sector perspectives. In the areas of art and design, practices around experiential and practice-led R&D (Mortensen Steagall et al., 2022; Scholtes & Batorowicz, 2019; Brooker, 2021) have crystallised into a widely adopted approach to innovation. Media research has focused on discussing R&D as a pathway to different typologies of innovation (Bleyen et al., 2014) – e.g. process and product innovation – and emerging concepts such as open innovation (Klaß, 2020). Research has also explored the shifting role of R&D in the film industry and its impact on VFX and animation/games (Gowanlock, 2021; Kultima & Peltoniemi, 2012), as well as the contrasting and specific forms of innovation that question the role of public intervention (Benghozi et al., 2017), and the link between innovation and productivity (Chen & Amahah, 2016). There are also studies exploring R&D in the book publishing sector (Benghozi & Salvador, 2016) and the museum sector (Chuan et al., 2023).

These studies provide useful evidence of how R&D leads to innovation, with less focus on how R&D processes work in practice. Studies addressing R&D processes across several sectors and countries (UK Innovation Survey, 2021) offer only limited evidence of R&D models and are mainly focused on medium and large companies, rather than micro-businesses and freelancers that form a large share of the creative industries (Easton & Beckett, 2021). The few studies exploring perceptual aspects of R&D in the creative industries tend to adopt a functional lens – i.e. one where the perceptual traits are analysed in function of the impact that they generate at the level of business departments (Tükenmez et al., 2017) and not in terms of how they can shape an overall vision of R&D.

Two main challenges emerge from the literature review. First, despite some progress, mainstream concepts and approaches to R&D remain restrictive and not reflective of the extent and nature of R&D processes in the creative industries. A suitable way of exploring the perception of R&D is by looking at what value is assigned by creative businesses to such processes, i.e. how accumulated knowledge is transformed into perceived benefits. It can cover tangible spillover effects such as returns (Hall et al., 2010), patents (Jaffe, 1986) and productivity (Pappas & Remer, 1985) but also less tangible value that cannot be easily monetised, such as process novelty, time effectiveness and market readiness levels of R&D projects. Furthermore, the complexity of R&D practices in the creative industries complicates the process of identifying typical R&D traits that help us to distinguish it from R&D in other sectors. *Nesta* (Lomas, 2017) specifically calls for further research that develops R&D case studies and sets up frameworks for evaluating such practices. In this context, the five criteria established by the *Frascati Manual* (novel, creative, uncertain, systematic and transferable) need to be further tested against empirical in-depth evidence about R&D process characteristics in the creative industries. Our study takes these two challenges as a point of departure, asking:

- How are R&D processes perceived in the creative industries in terms of the value that businesses assign to the concept and;
- Which perceptual characteristics distinguish these forms of R&D processes?

The value and characteristics of R&D

Assessing the perception of R&D

As we discussed in Chapter 1, the Clwstwr programme was designed to rethink R&D processes in ways that made them relevant and impactful for people working in the creative industries. In this section we look at what we can learn from this kind of initiative and assess the extent to which a Clwstwr style innovation ecosystem is perceived as useful and effective. We asked interviewees: how different R&D processes are to their day-to-day business activity; if the time invested in R&D processes was worth their effort; and if their expectations in terms of 'market readiness' levels of R&D outputs were met or not. The analysis and interviews led to the exploration of three areas:

1 process novelty,
2 time effectiveness and
3 market readiness.

Process novelty

Novelty is one of the defining traits of R&D. While research has explored the novelty of R&D and innovation outputs (see, e.g., Criscuolo et al., 2017; Janssen et al., 2015), less is known about the novelty that R&D introduces into creative industries' processes, i.e. how different R&D processes actually are from everyday business activities. We assessed the degree to which R&D undertaken in the frame of each Clwstwr project was different from the day-to-day business activity, coding responses based on a three-point Likert scale – high difference, medium difference and low difference.

Our responses show that 34% of respondents assign a high level of novelty to R&D practices within their businesses (Figure 2.1), 60% of respondents (45 businesses) assign a medium level of novelty and only 6% of respondents assign a low level of novelty to their R&D practices. These results suggest that for most businesses (94%), there is a clear distinction

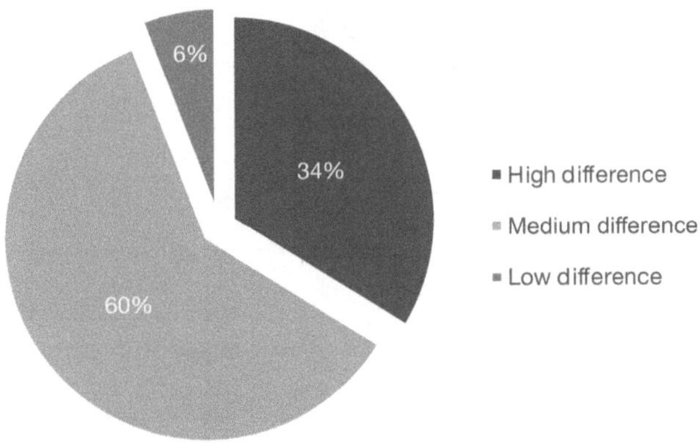

Figure 2.1 Degree of R&D process novelty perceived by creative industries businesses.

between their everyday activities and R&D, with only a small minority seeing R&D as part of business as usual. However, a majority of those who had taken part in R&D projects – the 60% who opted for the medium level of novelty – were able to see connections between their R&D projects and their everyday business activities.

Time effectiveness

R&D performance is traditionally measured through indicators such as productivity levels, financial performance or developed patents. We can also measure R&D performance by looking at the time and resources it absorbs – accomplishing R&D objectives within time and budget (Szakonyi, 1994), but also the extent to which time and resources devoted to R&D are seen as time well spent. This is complicated by the fact that the economic impact of R&D processes on businesses is not immediately visible and needs time and effort to materialise: a form of deferred gratification that will be important in shaping the perception of R&D for creative companies used to moving from one commission to the next.

We assessed how time-effective R&D processes are for creative businesses. The analysis reveals that (Figure 2.2) 93% of respondents responded positively asked whether R&D processes were worth the effort and time, with only 7% (5 out of 68 companies) replying more speculatively (with 'maybe'), and none of the respondents saying that they didn't consider invested time to be worth their effort. For the 7% less sure about the effectiveness of R&D, their uncertainty often came from the time lag between research, development and commercialisation. But in most cases,

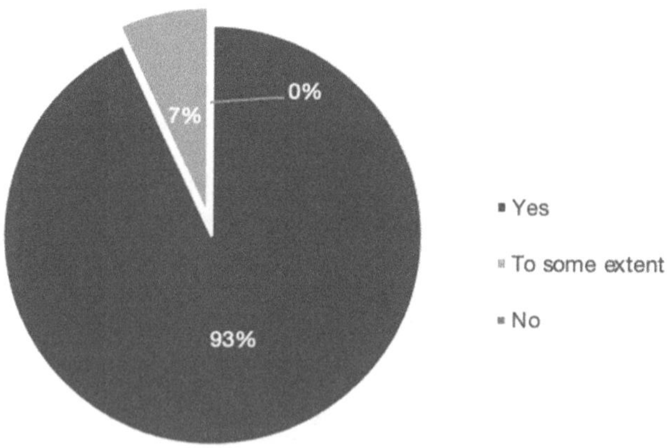

Figure 2.2 Degree of time effectiveness of R&D processes perceived by creative industries businesses.

these results vindicate efforts (like Clwstwr and the CICP programme) to find ways to develop R&D support structures for the creative industries.

Market readiness

Market readiness of R&D process outcomes is a routine process for measuring R&D value. A universally deployed tool for measuring the market readiness of products, services and experiences are Technology Readiness Levels (TRLs) scale (EC, 2014). Although conceived for the technology-based sectors, TRLs can be conceptually redeployed for other sectors (Van Cauwenbergh et al., 2022). For the creative industries, TRLs can be used to measure how far companies were able to travel on their R&D projects (to, e.g., the production of a proof of concept, prototypes or market-ready solutions).

While TRLs are common in the tech industry to measure the maturity of innovative technologies, many of the companies involved were focused on less technical forms of innovation – in areas like storytelling or business models – so we asked businesses to consider the readiness levels of their projects more broadly. Indeed, we would suggest that while TRLs are useful as indicators of R&D journeys, replacing the word technology with a broader term – such as outputs – might be more useful. We assessed perceptions of R&D through the lens of their expectations (in terms of market readiness of R&D), measuring how mature their R&D outputs were perceived to be. Once we redefined the meaning of 'technology' – to include any creative output – we were able to use a traditional TRL (or Output Readiness Level) structure, with respondents assessing their solutions from a scale from 1 to 9 (1–3: proof of concept; 4–6: prototype; 7–9 fully marketable solution). We asked them to assess which TRL/ORL level they set out to achieve at the start of their projects and compared this to the level they reached at the end of their project. Only five projects could not ascribe their projects to a level of maturity, as the nature of their solution was too difficult to align to the TRL scale. Most projects, once the TRL terminology was translated to include the range of creative industries outputs, were able to assess where their projects fitted on the TRL scale.

Results show a fairly even spread between the number of projects falling within each of the three development stages, with the last development stage (TRL 7–9) slightly larger than the others (Figure 2.3). Given the comparatively modest levels of funding for R&D projects and the speculative nature of many projects involved in the Clwstwr programme, this suggests that many companies were able to move through the stages fairly quickly. It also indicates a fairly high degree of success for the programme as a whole, with companies embracing R&D as a viable route to innovation.

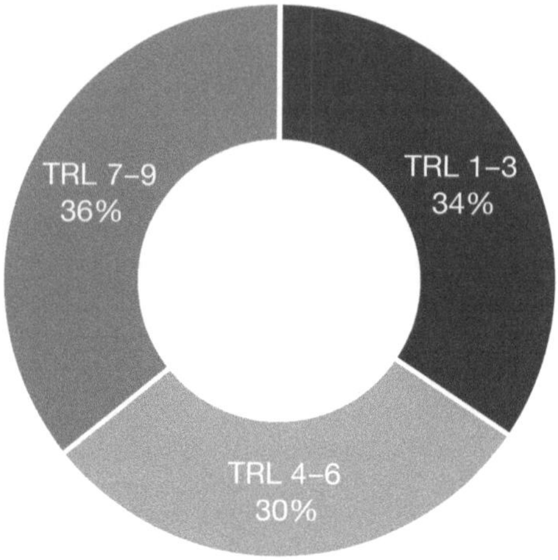

Figure 2.3 Degree of TRL levels outcome of R&D processes as perceived by creative industries businesses.

When we compared this against prior expectations, our analysis shows that over half of the companies achieved the stage they set out to, indicating – given the inherently speculative nature of R&D – a strong level of performance against objectives. Only 21% of respondents failed to reach their expected levels of market readiness – a surprisingly low failure rate for such an experimental initiative (Figure 2.4).

Overall, these results suggest that:

1 R&D is still far from becoming common practice in the creative industries, with only 6% of those taking part in the Clwstwr programme seeing its structure and mechanisms as part of their day-to-day activities. Nonetheless, most of those involved – 60% – were able to relate their R&D activity to their day-to-day business.
2 There is a strong affirmation of the importance of R&D for creative businesses, despite the high risks involved and the – sometimes – slow return on investment. Given that the creative industries are often a project-based, freelance domain, in high need of stable income, this result enforces the potential value and long-term effects that creative businesses see in implementing R&D.

Characteristics of R&D

Building on these findings, we set out to assess if a unified, conceptual model of understanding R&D processes in the creative industries is

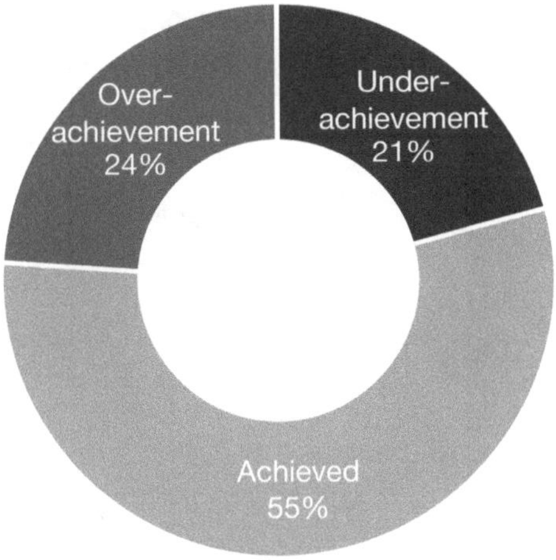

Figure 2.4 Achievement of market readiness levels.

possible and, if so, outline its defining traits. We conducted a qualitative analysis of our interview transcripts to explore how value assessment can create new insights into R&D traits that are typical for the creative industries. We coded the responses of all interviews, extracting data that referred to the perceived nature and mechanisms of R&D processes. Together, the analysis of value assignment and typical characteristics of R&D provides a more complete overview of how R&D is understood and practised within the creative industries. The qualitative findings presented below allowed us to identify seven distinct characteristics of creative industries R&D. These are grouped into two categories: core traits (commonly identified characteristics) and secondary traits (present, but less commonly identified characteristics) (Figure 2.5).

1 ***An iterative process***
   This characteristic refers to the experience of R&D processes as cyclic – and often repetitive – rather than linear. This favours small, explorative steps rather than larger, bolder moves, as they enable creative businesses to test the ground and take fewer risks. While the standard approach to conducting research sees first a phase of methodological definition, followed by a data collection phase and data analysis, creative businesses see the R&D process as more fragmented and cyclical (in line with the classic 'double diamond' approach used on User-Centred Design). Methodologies and research tools were often adjusted after initial tests and trials, reflecting the needs and complexity of the R&D, as well as shifting context and conditions. A good

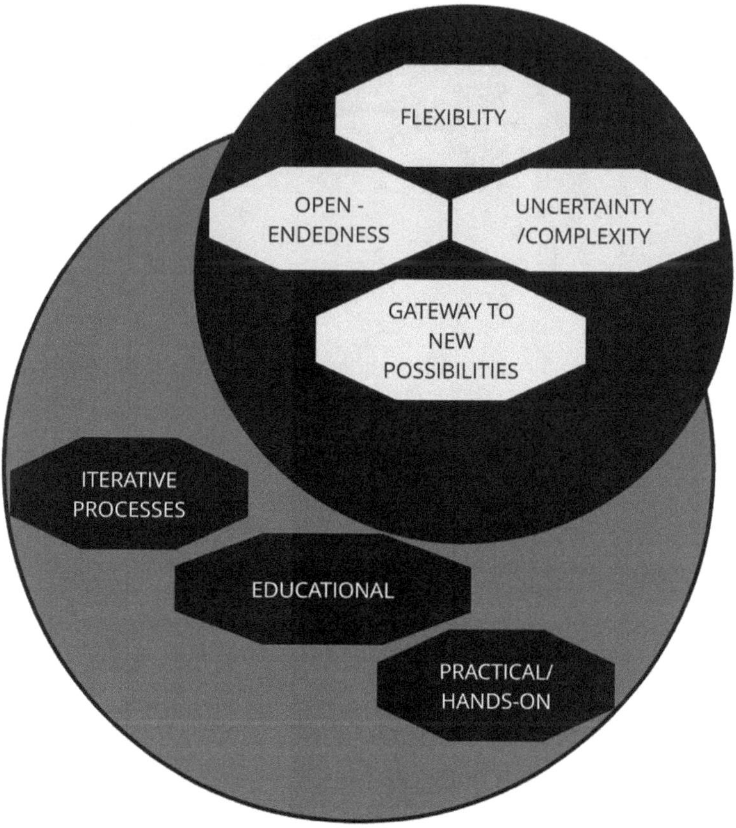

Figure 2.5 Conceptual model highlighting characteristics of R&D processes in the creative industries.

example is the pathway followed by the company *Bombastic*, which was exploring digital learning solutions for schools:

> We started our user tests, developing the tech in quite a positive way, but of course reasonably after a few months, of course, we hit low because of the pandemic. (…) We actually really had the opportunity to reimagine our product for remote learning situations because of the pandemic. (…) Through the early months of the pandemic we reformulated our objectives and ideas to actually transpose our interactive platform for an online teaching experience. So that was very positive. And we saw that meant we could still continue researching and developing our project.

The cyclical approach is designed to allow progressive development towards an appropriate solution to a challenge, with each phase bringing improvements before the next phase. This approach benefits from close monitoring, evaluation and reflection on each stage. *Lewnah* – a company aiming to develop an engaging news programme for children – describes how this introduces layers of uncertainty into the process:

> It was difficult to keep on track because an R&D process inevitably will change as you go on; your final budget will almost certainly look very different to what you predicted at the start.

Several companies stressed the iterative nature of R&D processes during their interview. For example, *Little Bird*, aiming to improve the environmental sustainability of production companies, stressed the importance of conducting research iteratively and in small steps – a way of working that contrasts sharply with project/content development for most production companies. Similarly, *Monnow Media* – focussing on reimagining news journalism – saw the value of R&D as an investigative, iterative process, which requires a specific framework but allows flexibility. The manager of *For Cardiff* explained how, for them, different iterations were necessary to find working solutions when reaching dead-ends, with methods and tools changing to reflect new iterations.

2 ***Uncertainty/complexity***

R&D processes are often complex and always uncertain with many unknown variables (external and company-based) that can change during the course of the exploration. Speaking about their research process for developing an immersive news programme for children, *Lewnah* described how

> The R&D experience is never smooth from A to B; you sort of take ten steps forward, and then two steps back. It was very much like that for us.

For *Rescape* – exploring how VR technology can be developed in healthcare – the uncertainty and complexity of R&D required the integration of different perspectives. *Voice Wales Photo Agency* – aiming to research and develop a new kind of photo agency for the Welsh news industry – a major challenge of R&D is '*managing the days when you feel you're not getting anywhere*', but also the '*patience (required) in seeing the results emerge*'. Another interviewee explained that they had to adapt their normal working rhythm to another, slower one, fitting with the pace of R&D processes, while '*dealing with research outcomes that were not expected*' (*Caerphilly Observer*).

While uncertainty was undoubtedly challenging, some respondents – such as the project manager of *Edge21* – welcomed it:

> The uncertainty was really exciting. I quite liked the unknown and I dived straight into the unknown and embraced it (...), because Clwstwr and the R&D experience has been a massive turning point for me in my career.

The manager of *Goggleminds* – another project exploring the use of immersive technology in healthcare – describes how their capacity to deal with uncertainty and complexity grew as they moved from a Seed project to a second-phase development project:

> The second project was a lot more complex, because there was a lot more uncertainty, I would say. It was definitely more challenging but we've learned a lot from the first project, the team was growing so we were less reliant on contractors and we were much better placed. If we would have done the second project at the start, I think it would have been a different journey, not necessarily a different outcome, but a different journey.

Whether seen as a challenge or an obstacle, the degree of uncertainty and complexity of doing R&D processes pushed companies outside their normal business routines. Nonetheless, it was, for most, an intrinsic part of the experience.

3 ***Learning new skills***

Many projects saw learning as an important part of the process of addressing the specific problems or questions that framed their R&D. Several of the interviewed businesses confirmed that they learnt a great deal about the new field of exploration or discovered new methods and approaches for addressing their research questions. For example, the manager of *Goggleminds* discussed the accelerated learning curve for staff, which led to doubling the level of productivity and completing the second project in half the time. He also stressed the layered learning process involving different steps and approaches:

> A lot of the research we've done indoor endorsed in a way, and consolidated our thinking, from the outset. Before we thought we had done the research we sort of had to do the research to find out if we were heading in the right direction, so it was a real learning curve.

Other companies like *Ie Ie Productions (Candylion project)* reflected upon the need for a focused approach when performing R&D and acquiring new skills and knowledge:

> Learning about interactive film and gaming definitely opened up those worlds. It also gave us an opportunity to explore that, and also to do some work on the characters, to get the team back together to get them focused in a workshop and talking through a very long process. And those benefits of time to think and explore opportunities, and then decide actually 'no, we clearly need to stick to one thing', that's invaluable at the end of the day, instead of trying to go off trying to do too many things.

Learning also happens at different levels, as explained by managers of the *Laku Neg*, a project aiming to tell indigenous stories on screen:

> It's this whole idea of learning new software and learning new things, learning new pathways to do things, and I know that it was a learning journey for us in regards to that whole idea of how to go through the process, how to administer the process.

All the testimonials collected from funded R&D projects, in different ways, highlight the multiplicity of learning avenues and levels, as well as personal forms of defining learning outcomes.

4 *Practicality*

Interviewees stressed the need for practical R&D processes to obtain hands-on, applicable results. The project manager of the *Voice Wales Photo Agency* project reflected on the difference between fundamental and applied research. From her perspective, the first is theoretical, strongly framed by academic contexts, while the second has a practical finality and applicability for the development of creative solutions:

> I've got a bit distracted with other avenues which I don't know how relevant they were at that point in the process. I was looking at what photos mean to people and what it means to be Welsh and that kind of line of thought, but that was a lot academic kind of journals and stuff and I just didn't really know if I was on the right track with it, so I went to one of the like market research workshops. The workshop speaker was talking a lot about questionnaires and how you word your research question and I started thinking a lot about my question. And it was really useful actually because she kind of like got me back on track, because she told me that the pure academic side of things in this case, probably wasn't the most relevant and most useful use of my time and I should be looking if the market demand exists, and I could do this by doing compared searches between how many Welsh identity photos come up, based in Wales on certain topics and comparing it with a search on England and so doing those kind of research really helped me to get back on track.

The manager of *Lewnah* also made a distinction between R&D as a more theoretical and conceptual practice aimed at developing knowledge, and development as a concrete process aimed to deliver concrete results in the form of solutions. For her, this was articulated as moving from R&D to D&R:

> We were still conducting R&D, but it was more like instead of doing research and development, we were doing development and then research. So, the second stage of the project funding was very much about trying to develop a prototype, a tangible thing. And this is like: Let's actually produce a thing, a pilot that we can then go and do research and test on the market. So, it felt a little bit more straightforward .... Again, it was just having to interpret R&D for our own purposes.

5 ***Flexibility***

This trait is closely aligned to the iterative, uncertain nature of the process, and the need to adjust resources, focus and approaches during the R&D, based on progress instead of following a pre-established itinerary. This aspect is highlighted by the managers of *Agile Kinetic*:

> If you're doing real R&D and you learn things as you go along, when you need to be able to change the plan and Clwstwr let us do that. With Clwstwr it was more flexible, so we were able to kind of go where the research took us a lot more easily, which was great.

Flexibility is also among the identified traits of R&D processes identified by companies implementing such projects for the first time. For example, the manager of *Mapped Out* – a news journalism project targeting neurodivergent audiences – told us that

> R&D offers more time to think, to explore, to follow instincts and trial things; it is an open and flexible process.

6 ***Open-endedness***

Often used in conjunction with flexibility, the concept of open-endedness identifies the lack of rigid boundaries of R&D processes. It also marks the possibility of future changes, as well as the broadness and unrestricted nature of such processes. The broad variety of associations of the concept with benefits or challenges was identified by respondents in different ways throughout the interviews. Positive reflections on open-endedness were linked with freedom and the ability to explore new avenues:

> The R&D was incredibly freeing because you could just play with the possibilities. It wasn't: you have to deliver X, it was sort of there's going to be an x but we don't know what that's going to look like. Compared to any other work, it was probably the most freeing experience for me as a practitioner.
>
> (Edge21)

Other respondents saw open-endedness as a form of empowerment. The manager of the *Tredboy* project, who was using R&D for the first time, told us that

> The core difference was that instead of being results-based or product-based R&D is more open-ended and therefore empowering.

Respondents who were more familiar with R&D processes, such as the manager of the *Object Matrix* project – saw this as simply built-in to the process:

> R&D is a more open-ended and flexible process, informed by findings rather than pre-established.

But this open-endedness was, for many, a real challenge. The manager of the *Candylion* project told us that R&D

> offered time and space to explore opportunities and do the necessary research but (is) also challenging because it is so open-ended.

For some, the concept of open-endedness stands in contrast to everyday business operations. *Martha Stone Productions*, who were exploring online interactive training possibilities, explained how they

> had to go through a completely new process that is not similar to producing a TV documentary, but open-ended.

7 ***Gateway to new possibilities***

For some of our respondents, applying R&D processes in the creative industries is seen as a *gateway to new possibilities*. These change during the course of a project, a point made by the project manager of *Nimble Productions*, a company aiming to develop content for women's football:

> Doing this process, what none of us had anticipated, was that it moved away from our initial idea. Having a co-investigator and a

> producer, thus an extra level of support enabled us to get the initial desk research done, to hold the focus groups, to get access to two schools and just checking that we were pitching things at the right level of wording, and made us actually change the direction of the project which none of us were anticipating at the start.

In the same vein, *Monnow Media*, a company exploring modular journalism, explained that the time dedicated to R&D led to developing new ideas and exploring different avenues for radically new ways of doing journalism. The new possibilities opened up by R&D could cross domains, enriching and providing novel and surprising outcomes, as the manager of *The Democracy Box* project explains:

> The R&D project allowed me to take my work into a different sector. I can't quite explain the impact of it. I didn't even know there was a democracy sector. It allowed me to research that, map it and create a bridge from the arts & cultural sector to democracy.

However, the broad range of exploration possibilities offered by R&D processes comes with constraints and costs. The project manager of *Martha Stone*, speaking about the way that R&D provides new avenues to develop products, was also aware of the need to extend funding streams to be able to explore new, previously unanticipated possibilities.

Conclusions

Our purpose, in this chapter, is not to substitute but to complement existing instruments and studies to provide more granularity in the way we understand R&D processes in the creative industries. Our findings show that

- A clear majority – 93% of respondents – believe that R&D is worth the investment of time and resources. Despite the built-in uncertainty, most Clwstwr projects achieved a (TRL) level of progress that met their expectations, with over a third reaching the later stages of readiness levels.
- R&D is still a novel and unfamiliar process for most creative companies – 94% of respondents assign a high or medium level of novelty to the R&D process. This is reflected in our qualitative analysis of interviews with project leads, with many commenting on various ways in which novelty and uncertainty were an inherent part of their R&D experience.

We have identified 7 R&D traits that emerge from our interviews with creative businesses and freelancers (both core and secondary). Many of these – uncertainty, open-endedness, the need for learning, the discovery of new possibilities – require the kind of time and resources that most creative businesses have typically had little access to, pointing to the need for both external funding and support systems to guide companies through the complex terrain of R&D. Our interviews suggest that the potential rewards show that investment in creative industries R&D can become a routine part of innovation policy and practice.

References

Bakhshi, H. (2022). The art of R&D. Creative Industries Policy and Evidence Centre Report. https://pec.ac.uk/research-reports/the-art-of-r-and-d. ISBN: 978-1-913095-59-8

Bakhshi, H. Breckon, J., & Puttick, R. (2021). Understanding R&D in the arts, humanities and social sciences. *Journal of the British Academy*, 9, 115–145. https://doi.org/10.5871/jba/009.115

Bakhshi, H., & Lomas, E. (2017). *Defining R&D for the creative industries*. Policy Brief, London: Nesta.

Benghozi, P.-J., & Salvador, E. (2016). How and where R&D takes place in creative industries? Digital investment strategies of the book publishing sector. *Technology Analysis & Strategic Management*, *28*(5), 568–582. https://doi.org/10.1080/09537325.2015.1122184

Benghozi, P. J., Salvador, E., and Simon, J. P. (2017). The race for innovation in the media and content industries: Legacy players and newcomers: Lessons for policy makers from the video game and cinema industries. *The Journal of Arts Management, Law, and Society*, *47*(5), 346–360. https://doi.org/10.1080/10632921.2017.1366382

Bleyen, V.-A., Lindmark, S., Ranaivoson, H., & Ballon, P. (2014). A typology of media innovations: Insights from an exploratory study. *The Journal of Media Innovations*, *1*(1), 28–51. https://doi.org/10.5617/jmi.v1i1.800

Brooker, G. (2021). Site: An inventories approach to practice-led research. In C. Vear (Ed.), *The Routledge International handbook of practice-based research* (pp. 398–414). London: Routledge. ISBN: 0367341433

Chen, J., & Amahah, J. (2016). Cultural industries and innovation-an empirical analysis. *ICEB 2016 Proceedings (Xiamen, China)*. 75. https://aisel.aisnet.org/iceb2016/75

Chuan, L., Coll-Serrano, V., & Rausell-Köster, P. (2023). Exploring the evidence-based driving factors of innovation in arts and cultural organizations. *Empirical Studies of the Arts*. https://doi.org/10.1177/02762374231155746

Criscuolo, P., Dahlander, L., Grohsjean, T., & Salter, A. (2017). Evaluating novelty: The role of panels in the selection of R&D projects. *Academy of Management Journal*, *60*(2), 433–460. https://doi.org/10.2139/ssrn.3650896

Easton, E., & Beckett, B. (2021). Freelancers in the creative industries. Creative Industries Policy & Evidence Centre. Available from: https://pec.ac.uk/policy-briefings/freelancers-in-the-creative-industries. (Accessed on 24/02/2024).

European Commission (EC) (2014). Technology readiness levels (TRL), HORIZON 2020 – WORK PROGRAMME 2014–2015, General Annexes. Available online at: https://ec.europa.eu/research/participants/data/ref/h2020/wp/2014_2015/annexes/h2020-wp1415-annex-g-trl_en.pdf (Accessed on 24/02/2024).

Gowanlock, J. (2021). Animating unpredictable effects: Nonlinearity in Hollywood's R&D complex. *Springer Nature*. https://doi.org/10.1007/978-3-030-74227-0

Hall, B. H., Mairesse, J., & Mohnen, P. (2010). Measuring the returns to R&D. In B. Hall, & N. Rosenberg (Eds.), *Handbook of the economics of innovation* (Vol. 2, pp. 1033–1082). London: Elsevier and North-Holland. ISBN: 9780444519955.

Jaffe, A. B. (1986). Technological opportunity and spillovers of R&D: Evidence from firms' patents, profits and market value. https://doi.org/10.3386/w1815

Janssen, M., Stoopendaal, A. M., & Putters, K. (2015). Situated novelty: Introducing a process perspective on the study of innovation. *Research Policy*, *44*(10), 1974–1984. https://doi.org/10.1016/j.respol.2015.06.008

Kaleniuk, I., & Kuznetsova, N. (2022). Creative economy in the global innovation process. *International Economic Policy*, *36*, 92–114. https://doi.org/10.33111/iep.2022.36.05

Klaß, N. (2020). Open innovation in media innovation research – A systematic literature review. *Journal of Media Business Studies*, *17*(2), 190–218. https://doi.org/10.1080/16522354.2020.1724498

Kultima, A., & Peltoniemi, M. (2012). Games and Innovation Research Seminar. 2011 Working Papers. ISBN 978-951-44-8705-7. https://trepo.tuni.fi/bitstream/handle/10024/65771/games_and_innovation_research_2012.pdf?sequence=1

Lomas, E. (2017). Defining R&D for the arts and knowledge cultural domains. UCL, Available at: https://discovery.ucl.ac.uk/id/eprint/1543295/1/R%26D_FinalReport_elomas_ahrc_ucl_2017.pdf (Accessed on 24/02/2023).

Mortensen Steagall, M., Massarolo, J., Gallo, S. N., & Grieve, F. (2022). *The link 2022 journal: A collection on practice-led research*. ISSN: 1279-1465.

Nesta. (2006). *The innovation gap: Why policy needs to reflect the reality of innovation in the UK*. London: Nesta.

OECD, Manual, Frascati. (2015). Guidelines for collecting and reporting data on research and experimental development. Available at: http://www.oecd.org/sti/frascati-manual-2015-9789264239012-en.htm (Accessed on 22/02/2024).

Pappas, R. A., & Remer, D. S. (1985). Measuring R&D productivity. *Research Management*, *28*(3), 15–22. https://doi.org/10.1080/00345334.1985.11756896

R&D in the Creative Industries Survey. (2020). UK Government, Department for Culture, Media & Sport, Available at: https://www.gov.uk/government/publications/rd-in-the-creative-industries-survey/rd-in-the-creative-industries-survey#:~:text=However%2C%20there%20is%20also%20evidence,innovation%20in%20processes%20and%20products (Accessed on 24/02/2024).

Scholtes, M., & Batorowicz, B. (2019). *Practice-led research and the myth of rigour*. NiTRO: Non-Traditional Research Outcomes. Available at: https://research.usq.edu.au/item/q5643/practice-led-research-and-the-myth-of-rigour

Schumpeter, J. (1912/1934). *The theory of economic development*. Cambridge, MA: Harvard University Press. https://doi.org/10.4324/9781315135564

Siepel, J., Bakshi, H., Bloom, M., & Ospina, J. V. (2022). Understanding Createch R&D, Nesta. Available online at: https://cdn2.assets-servd.host/creative-pec/production/assets/images/PEC-Understanding-Createch-RD-December-2022.pdf (Accessed on 24/02/2024).

Szakonyi, R. (1994). Measuring R&D effectiveness—I. *Research-Technology Management*, *37*(2), 27–32. https://doi.org/10.1080/08956308.1994.11670966

Tükenmez, A., Durmaz, Y., & Aslan, Z. (2017). Company employees' perception of R&D and perception's effect on departments. Şirket Çalışanlarının AR-GE Algısı ve Departmanlar Üzerindeki Etkisi (Teknopark Uygulaması). *AURUM Mühendislik Sistemleri ve Mimarlık Dergisi*, *1*(2), 31–40. https://hdl.handle.net/20.500.12939/1916

UK Innovation Survey. (2021). UK Government, Department for Business, Energy & Industrial Strategy. Available at: https://assets.publishing.service.gov.uk/government/uploads/system/uploads/attachment_data/file/1074069/UK_Innovation_Survey_2021_Report.pdf (Accessed on 24/02/2024).

Van Cauwenbergh, N., Dourojeanni, P. A., van der Zaag, P., Brugnach, M., Dartee, K., Giordano, R., & Lopez-Gunn, E. (2022). Beyond TRL–Understanding institutional readiness for implementation of nature-based solutions. *Environmental Science & Policy*, *127*, 293–302. https://doi.org/10.1016/j.envsci.2021.09.021

3 Identifying innovation

A new typology for the creative industries

Marlen Komorowski

Why do we need a new innovation typology?

The OECD's *Oslo Manual* defines an innovation as: "a new or improved product or process (or combination thereof) that differs significantly from the unit's previous products or processes and that has been made available to potential users (product) or brought into use by the unit (process)" (OECD & Eurostat, 2018). But the OECD definition of innovation, while valuable, struggles to capture the full spectrum of innovation types in the creative industries. So, for example:

- A theatre troupe might continuously refine a production over multiple seasons. While these refinements tend to be gradual rather than radical, the iterative nature of this process leads to a constantly evolving experience that challenges the "new or improved" aspect of the definition.
- Virtual Reality (VR) experiences can transport users to new worlds or historical periods, creating a sense of novelty through immersive storytelling. But the innovation is as likely to be about narrative as it is about technology, making VR experiences difficult to quantify within the OECD framework.
- A game developer creates a mobile app that combines entertainment with educational elements on climate change. The innovative element here is the creation of a novel learning experience with a social purpose.
- In television, some of the most valuable intellectual property is around new formats, which can be licensed to be remade in other countries. New formats, while partly derivative (as much innovation is), may not involve innovation as described above at all.

These examples show the extent to which innovation in the creative industries can take a variety of forms that are usually not captured by existing typologies. There is still a lack of understanding of the relationship and

DOI: 10.4324/9781003481805-3
This chapter has been made available under a CC BY-NC-ND 4.0 license.

interdependence between different kinds of innovation and the creative industries (see also Chapter 1). It is also important to consider what constitutes innovation in the creative industries to understand different innovation types. And, these distinctions between the creative industries and other industries mean that the kinds of innovation that creative industries businesses and employees undertake differ in significant ways.

The purpose of this chapter, building on Chapter 2, is to provide a new typology of innovation in the creative industries. The new typology was developed following an analysis of interviews with 68 freelancers or businesses, funded and supported by Clwstwr to conduct R&D, as part of UK's CICP (see Chapter 1 for more details about the methodology). We begin with a literature review of existing typologies of innovation and an analysis of their limited applicability for the creative industries. This informs our findings, which enable us to present a new typology for innovation in the creative industries. Finally, we discuss how this new typology can impact creative businesses, future research, and policy.

Innovation types and classification systems

The development of innovation types and classifications has become a central focus of academic inquiry (Chandy & Prabhu, 2010; Cinar et al., 2024; Garcia & Calantone, 2002; Knüpling et al., 2022) and policy development (OECD & Eurostat, 2018). To navigate the concept of innovation, researchers and practitioners have devised various typologies. These range from simple labels like 'radical' or 'incremental' to more elaborate typologies that differentiate innovation types or identify distinct profiles of innovators (Knüpling et al., 2022). Authors have stressed a lack of consistent dimensions for constructing an understanding of innovation and different types of innovation (Garcia & Calantone, 2002). Available classifications of innovation have been also criticised for their lack of coherence and consistency across existing frameworks (e.g. Schartinger et al., 2022).

For example, the OECD's *Frascati Manual* (OECD, 2015) divides innovation into three categories: fundamental, applied, and experimental development (see also Chapter 2). This classification is largely based on how close research is to being used in a commercial setting. Kovacs et al. (2019), following a systematic literature review, proposed using novelty and impact to categorise innovation. While these dimensions are useful for creating quantifiable measures of innovation, it has been argued that they don't fully capture the nuances of all types of innovation (Knüpling et al., 2022).

The overarching aim of these typologies is twofold. First, they aim to bring clarity and structure to innovation. By categorising innovation based on specific characteristics, researchers can identify patterns, analyse trends, and conduct comparative studies (Cinar et al., 2024). Second, these typologies serve as practical tools. Policymakers can leverage them to design targeted support structures for different innovation streams, while firms can utilise them to develop innovation strategies tailored to their specific goals (Knüpling et al., 2022). The data and research underpinning innovation classifications typically stem from a range of sources, including innovation surveys, patent analysis, and bibliometric studies. Additionally, sector-specific reports and case studies can provide a deeper understanding of innovation dynamics within industries.

To our knowledge, no studies have yet attempted to characterise innovation in the creative industries (see also Cinar et al., 2024). This is partly because the creative industries display unique characteristics (especially in contrast to the science and technology sectors) and because they have only become central to innovation policy comparatively recently (see also Chapter 1). We can identify various problems with existing typologies of innovation in the creative industries.

1 Current classifications tend to overemphasise a purely linear conception of novelty. As discussed above, the degree of novelty for creative industries' services and products is difficult to grasp but important. Creative industries thrive on an iterative process where creators continuously refine and adapt their work based on feedback, trends, and evolving cultural contexts. This iterative approach is fundamental to creative practices (see also Chapter 2). In the creative industries, dynamic processes of creativity and the often-essential role of end-users are central throughout all production (and not only to innovation). This iterative approach, highlighted by Wölbling et al. (2012), is pivotal. But, in the creative industries, innovation can also be manifested through incremental improvements, reinterpretations, or novel combinations of existing elements (Gustafsson & Lazzaro, 2021). This makes an emphasis on novelty – particularly in its linear forms – sometimes difficult to operationalise in creative industries' innovation.
2 Existing typologies often see innovation only through the lens of technological advancement – while creative industries innovation encompasses various other forms. So, for example, innovation is measured typically through an index of 'technology readiness levels' (see also Chapter 2). Technological advancements certainly play a role in creative industries' innovation (e.g. digital music production or 3D printing). But innovation in the creative industries can include aesthetic innovation, cultural reinterpretation, and creative expressions, for example (Snowball et al., 2022). These forms of innovation are often intangible. Indeed, Miles and Green (2008) argue that in the creative industries, so-called 'hidden' innovations are much more common, making them distinct from more tangible technological innovations.

This includes, for example, innovation in organisational forms or business models and novel combinations of existing technologies and processes to produce creative outputs. Hence, in Chapter 2, we suggest replacing Technology Readiness Levels with a much broader term, such as Output Readiness Levels.

3 As we have suggested in Chapters 1 and 2, the current forms of language used to classify innovations are often a barrier for the creative industries. For example, the *Frascati Manual* relies on language rooted in scientific and technical contexts derived from STEM (science, technology, engineering, and mathematics) skillsets and related product markets (OECD, 2015). When Lomas (2017) analysed how the *Frascati Manual* might be applied to arts and culture, she found various terms used in the innovation survey by the OECD, and its studies are either not understood or cannot be applied to innovation in arts and culture. For example, there are rarely R&D-related roles or positions or dedicated spending on R&D in arts and cultural organisations – even though activities leading towards innovation in the creative industries can be classified as R&D. When applied to creative industries, this language may not resonate with the diverse actors, including artists, designers, and cultural practitioners, who contribute to innovation in these industries. Since policy funding and support are also often based on such terminology, this works to exclude creative industries organisations.

4 The focus on quantifiable outputs and measurable R&D activities in existing classification frameworks often overlooks the creative processes, social impact, and cultural value generation that are central to innovation in the creative industries (Gustafsson & Lazzaro, 2021). While economic growth (also driven by creative industries' innovation) has measurable indicators, it is much more difficult to quantify cultural and social values. Furthermore, metrics like patents or research publications are less relevant for creative industries. Innovation in creative industries often occurs through tacit knowledge, cultural expressions, and collective practices. The OECD, for example, measures R&D intensity based on the ratio of R&D expenditure to an output measure (Galindo-Rueda & Verger, 2016). However, most creative industries organisations don't classify R&D expenditure. The social and cultural value generated by creative innovation often defies easy quantification, leading to a significant underestimation of the creative industries' innovative capacity.

5 Finally, traditional innovation classifications are mostly rooted in explicit knowledge and therefore struggle to account for the intuitive and experiential dimensions of creativity and the learning involved. Creative industries thrive on tacit knowledge, which can include, for example, insights, intuition, and craft-based skills (Snowball et al., 2022).

These aspects are often difficult to codify or express explicitly. The collaborative nature of innovation is also difficult to grasp through existing classifications but is crucial for innovation in the creative industries (Gustafsson & Lazzaro, 2021).

In summary, we need to develop a new approach to classifying innovation in the creative industries that appreciates the context-specific aspects. By acknowledging the unique needs of innovators in the creative and cultural domain, we hope to develop a new understanding of innovation in the creative industries, supporting researchers and policymakers to encapsulate the complexities when designing innovation frameworks for the creative industries.

An innovation typology based on R&D processes

The two axes of R&D: Direction and degree of learning in innovation

In order to create a novel innovation typology for the creative industries, we analysed the interviews through a qualitative coding process. The analysis revealed that innovations in the creative industries can be best classified in terms of the R&D processes the creative industries projects go through in order to innovate. This enabled us to group the analysed projects across two opposing poles and two axes identifying the R&D process (Figure 3.1). The first axis describes the degree of pre-defined determination or R&D direction, which can rank from a highly focused and goal-oriented to a more open-ended and exploratory R&D process. The second axis describes the degree of learning throughout the R&D process, which ranges from refining existing knowledge and applying it to solve specific problems to acquiring new knowledge with the potential to open up completely new (and hitherto unknown) opportunities.

Our analysis enables us to score the R&D direction of each project in the creative industries on a scale from 1 (structured – representing the lowest level of flexibility and openness of the R&D process) to 4 (exploratory – the highest level of flexibility and openness of the R&D process). For the vertical axis – the learning curve achieved while conducting R&D – we compared the narratives used by interviewees against a specific question that asked them to assess the upskilling process of their teams while running the project. Where quantifiable data was not possible to obtain (17 out of 68 interviewees could not quantify their answer to this specific question), we used qualitative data generated from the graph narratives to score the levels of learning obtained during project implementation.

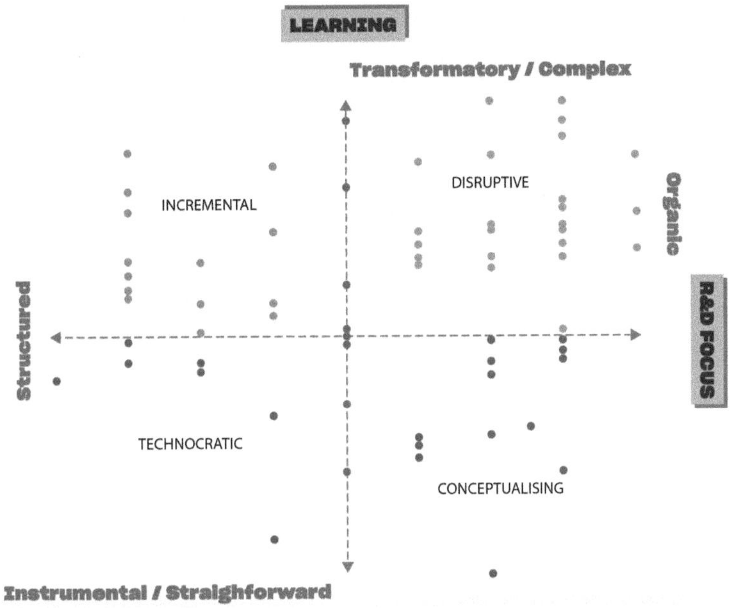

Figure 3.1 Types of innovation in the creative industries based on R&D processes.

The intersection of the two axes gave rise to four areas that define four different types of innovation in the creative industries, which can be graphically represented through a bubble graph (Figure 3.1). In the following section we describe the graph structure and the four types of innovation in the creative industries emerging from it. We give examples of each type of innovation through specific case studies of innovation projects.

1 ***Direction of R&D: Structured vs. exploratory***
The direction of R&D refers to the level of structure and discipline applied to the R&D process. Clwstwr's R&D projects showed various degrees of this and can be broadly differentiated into two groups. On the one hand, projects followed a set of structured R&D processes. This aligns with the concept of 'closed innovation' (Chesbrough, 2003), where R&D activities are primarily internal and tightly focused on addressing specific challenges. Here, the direction of R&D is predetermined and closely monitored. Research by Enkel et al. (2009) suggests limitations to this approach, as a purely exploitative approach in innovation management can lead to competency traps, where a focus on refining existing knowledge can hinder the exploration of new

creative territories. Hence, this kind of R&D process focuses on efficiently executing a predetermined vision, potentially utilising established production techniques and materials. It emphasises the exploitation of existing knowledge to create commercially viable products that cater to a well-defined target market.

A good example of how this kind of R&D works is provided by Bumpybox, a company funded by Clwtwr to explore how the efficiency of animation pipelines could be improved in order to grow the value of IP. The projects implemented by Bumpybox show an iterative and structured R&D process where small technical elements are being explored and tested out in a closed environment. The project manager of Bumpybox explained during the interview how the R&D process functioned:

> We've never done any R&D before, especially what I would call funded R&D (…). The premise of our project was that we were trying to make these animation shows, but were not getting much in terms of any other kind of licensing deal and the shows weren't expanding beyond TV. What we were trying to do is identify what we need to do to make our shows start to edge towards that with less funding. (…) So what we need to be doing is making this sort of brand appropriate and having material to show on the Internet, on social media, send prototypes to companies, while we're actually in production. So it was the first sort of line where it fully met expectations with the seed funding, because we tried lots of different things, and they all basically worked as we intended (…). We were trying lots of different small things and each had a success to it and that's why it met expectations, because we were in line with what we already knew we wanted to explore. That was pretty straightforward R&D where we tried all these things that were going by default. (…) Then we started our second project, where we were looking at the use of Metadata. Here, the major roadblock we had was that the amount of metadata that you needed to become useful is basically more than the material we had. We followed that sort of R&D path and exploration, which wasn't a failure because it works. We've implemented it in our pipeline, we've got the code for it, but at that moment what it needed to do or prove, it didn't really work. We then switched to one of the other elements of our R&D which was the use of Unreal Engine. It really opened a few doors and that's why it fully met expectations at the end.

For Bumpybox, this approach clearly delivered the kind of innovation they needed. For other Clwstwr projects, it was important to maintain high levels of exploration and flexibility in their R&D process.

They followed more open-ended R&D processes that were more exploratory and less rigidly structured. It allows for 'open innovation' (Chesbrough, 2003), where external knowledge and collaboration play a role in the R&D process. This openness can lead to the discovery of unexpected opportunities and the emergence of entirely new creative forms. The openness of the R&D process aligns with the concept of user-centred design (Von Hippel, 2005), where user needs and feedback heavily influence the innovation journey. In the creative industries, this can involve incorporating audience expectations and feedback into the R&D process, potentially leading to the development of more innovative and engaging creative experiences. Research by Gassmann and Schweitzer (2014) suggests that open innovation approaches can be particularly beneficial for radical innovation within creative industries. At the same time, there can be high rates of failure.

A good example of this type of R&D is provided by a freelancer working on a Clwstwr project, whose project focused on using a hybrid narrative, a new approach to filmmaking that combines illustration, graphic design, propaganda poster-style art, and live-action drama to improve the sustainability of filmmaking. The R&D process in this case was open-ended and more exploratory, enabling unexpected impacts to emerge. During the interview, the project lead explained this kind of process:

> I was looking at piloting something and trying a different way of making something. (…) I think that distinction between content creation and innovation is the way that the R&D community and the creative community might view each other with scepticism. I think the reality is actually a lot more blurred between them, and you can have stuff that is much purer content creation, but there is a place between them both where you know the material created points towards a new way of working in a new way of doing things. I think it's quite hard sometimes, for content creators, and the funders of content to naturally see the match between what could be purely technical R&D. So if there is content within it, and you get a sense of that, then all of a sudden it opens a lot of doors to show the potential of whatever is being done (…). Another big revelation was that the process is not about failure. It doesn't matter if the idea doesn't work out the way I thought it would, or if it leads somewhere else, because it's about what's discovered. This is very important in a field like film, which is highly judgmental and risk averse.

2 *Learning through R&D: Incremental vs. discovery*

The level of learning throughout the R&D process, as identified in the creative industries' innovation projects we analysed, captures the extent to which knowledge acquisition and refinement occur throughout the R&D process. Existing innovation literature differentiates between incremental and radical innovation (Anderson & Tushman, 2018), with the former focusing on improvements to existing products or services and the latter involving significant departures. While our typology acknowledges the potential for novelty in the outcome, it primarily focuses on the R&D process itself, particularly the level of learning throughout the process.

One end of the spectrum is characterised by a focus on refining existing knowledge. This aligns with the concept of exploitative learning (March, 1991). Here, the R&D process emphasises leveraging established knowledge and expertise to optimise existing practices and enhance efficiency. This approach prioritises the exploitation of existing knowledge for efficient problem-solving and product development. Research by Cohen et al. (2000) suggests that exploitative learning plays a vital role in incremental innovation. This aligns well with the creative industries, where many businesses may refine existing creative practices to cater to specific audience needs or adapt to evolving market trends. A good example of leveraging knowledge for product development is *Tunnel Vision*. The project explored how new and emerging technologies can enhance the public transport passenger experience, through the delivery of audio, video, and text content that is geospatially and contextually aware of passengers' needs. The manager of the project explained how the R&D process worked and the type of knowledge applied to develop the service prototype:

> The process involved two areas of research: The technical track looked at the state of technology regarding the provision of geo-contextual data to a train, and forecasting where the technology was going to go. The audience track looked at what the different audience needs are on trains in Wales – what the best way to serve passengers is and what they'd want. The technical track began by looking at who operates trains in Wales. We also looked at WiFi provision in stations and the uptake of digital ticketing. The audience track involved talking to passenger transport groups in Wales. We did some interviews and then some focus groups with commuters and leisure travellers to understand what they'd most be interested in. We found that it's possible to provide contextual content to Wales' trains, but the technology is suboptimal. But then we've obtained a big insight that could be the basis of a very different business and shifted our research focus. Because of COVID, train travel will move into digital ticketing. And the insight that came from the research is that the railway ticket is going to tell you if someone is going to move from and to at a certain time of the day

> and I could offer you some sizzle products relevant to your trip whether that is discounted lunches or two for one tickets to the cinema or concert venue. It was about the fact that digital ticketing plus mobile devices can create a more spatially aware advertising environment.

The other end of the spectrum emphasises identifying and acquiring new knowledge with the potential to open up entirely new creative possibilities. This aligns with the concept of exploratory learning (March, 1991). Here, the R&D process prioritises experimentation, discovery, and venturing into uncharted creative territory. This approach prioritises the exploration of new knowledge domains with the potential to revolutionise existing practices and even redefine, for example, audience expectations. Research by Hardy and Dougherty (1997) highlights the importance of learning for radical innovation. By venturing into uncharted territory and acquiring new knowledge, creative industries can foster the development of entirely new creative forms that disrupt existing markets and redefine the boundaries of their respective industries. The project Aomame represents a good example of an explorative R&D process based on a steep learning curve. The project explored what art online might look like if it utilised existing technologies more imaginatively and avoided simply replicating the physical gallery experience. The manager of Aomame explained how the R&D process worked and how intensive learning and pushing the limits of the possible was an important component in trying to revolutionise the exhibition of online art:

> The learning curve was extremely steep, but that's the point of the project, to expose ourselves to this very steep learning curve and then respond to it. The best way to do that is with a practical project. So that's what we did. What we're doing is we're mixing the art world with the computer game world: two different ecosystems coming together that neither understand each other, nor have any engagement with each other. The difficulty is that there is no crossover in these areas. This was the challenge. It was a challenge, and it's something we're still addressing now. (…) I could see the potential in the project. I could see that and I was going to try and turn it into a business, and I could see also that there was immense benefit from learning the skill set and getting involved in this world, having this opportunity. (…) It allowed me to press down the knowledge I had acquired, and actually put it into application again, so that, although it was like a baptism of fire, it means that I can now develop these kinds of things. The learning was reinforced.

The four archetypes of innovation in the creative industries

Based on the two identified axes, representing the direction of R&D and the depth of learning, we have developed a typology of creative industries innovation. This typology identifies four distinct archetypes of R&D-driven innovation within the creative industries: (1) technocratic, (2) incremental, (3) conceptualising, and (4) disrupting.

1 ***Technocratic innovation: Exploitative Learning within a Structured R&D Framework***
Technocratic innovation represents the most structured and focused form of innovation within the creative industries. This resonates with the existing concept of exploitation-oriented innovation (Van de Ven & Ring, 2006), where the primary goal is to refine existing knowledge and apply it to solve well-defined problems. Technocratic innovation in the creative industries primarily engages in exploitative learning (March, 1991). They leverage their established knowledge base and expertise to develop solutions for pre-defined challenges within the creative industries. Technocratic innovation can be compared to solution-oriented innovation (Oberländer et al., 2021), focusing on the specific needs of the creative industries.

Case study: FIELDWORK

The aim of Fieldwork's feasibility study was to explore the application of digital design capabilities in promoting original artworks. The goal of live gallery visits is to give people a personable experience of artworks, connect with artists, and posit new perspectives. The project thus explored the potential for transposing such a live experience through digital means. The new digital solution/platform should enrich public interaction with art and artists, through purchases, enhancing the livelihoods of the creative practitioners making the works. In doing so, the project aimed to put the interest of independent artists at the core of the platform that combines the best interests of multiple service providers (the artists) with the interests of the users (buyers) via an experiential, digital interaction. As a result, the end platform could join the dots between the public and private sectors, drawing on the strengths of both, to build economic and cultural gains.

The R&D process was a structured one, framed by a concrete context provided by digital solutions applied within the artwork field, which could communicate the story of handmade products to potential buyers using an innovative digital design. Established knowledge around digital forums and applications for selling artworks was being leveraged in order to meet users' and product providers' expectations. What was being researched is the potential layers of interactivity that these digital solutions could offer to tackle the challenge, as well as what a commercialisation model of a potential new digital solution/platform could look like.

The research methods deployed for this were straightforward: desk research was combined with interviews conducted with sector specialists and potential co-producers. A lot of research already done consolidated the thinking of the main professionals involved in this project. However, the acquired knowledge left the impression that only the surface of the analysed problematic was being scratched. Therefore, managers had to make important decisions and steer research to keep it contained and heading in the desired direction. The feasibility study illustrated that there is, still, an appetite for providing and running a platform. However, it also underlined that sustained time and financial investment are needed in order to bring the idea from a conceptual to a real marketable product.

In terms of the learning curve, although the desk research was substantial, it consisted in opening up knowledge about a sector in which the company did not have specific expertise: the digital solution sector applied to the art world. This means that already existing information and knowledge were gathered in order to be able to make informed decisions about the potential solution. Learning was therefore more exploitative than explorative. In practical terms, this meant that the project did not reach the level of defining the specifics of a digital platform, but focused more on uncovering the ethos, tone, aim, and potential functionality of the platform. Learning took place in a context in which the development of digital communication solutions applied to the creative industries is not new. Different models of platforms for artists such as Etsy, Zazzle, Artalistic, and so on already provide real solutions for the art market. How to expand the limited interaction possibilities of such platforms and make them more inclusive and representative of artists' interests represents a pre-defined problematic within the creative sphere, which the feasibility study aimed to tackle by looking at the specifics of the Welsh art market and looking at how the platform could represent artists and manage the connections and logistics for them, in order to provide greater economic potential for their creative practices.

2 ***Incremental innovation: Exploring New Applications within a Structured Framework***

Incremental innovations share some similarities with technocratic innovation through the application of a structured R&D approach. However, such innovation incorporates a limited degree of exploration within this framework. This aligns with the concept of architectural innovation (Henderson & Clark, 1990), where existing knowledge is applied to new contexts or markets. Incremental innovations engage in a balanced approach between exploitative and exploratory learning. They leverage their existing knowledge base while also venturing into new application areas. Incremental innovation differs from exploratory innovation (Lichtenthaler, 2009) in the limited scope of their exploration. While exploratory innovation actively seeks entirely new knowledge domains, incremental innovation primarily focuses on applying existing knowledge to new contexts within the creative industries.

Case study: AMPLYFI

AMPLYFI is a Welsh company developing ways of gathering data through AI, deep search, and other advanced technologies, enabling their clients to gain new insights. As part of their Clwstwr-funded project, AMPLYFI explored how AI could help journalism tackle some of the daily challenges in terms of big data and validation of sources. The company worked closely with journalists to use machine-learning and natural-language-processing capabilities to develop a tool to support story research by making connections between topics, people, organisations, and locations from across millions of documents. A key focus of the project was to ensure that this technology could be applied to a journalism use case and to increase the usability of the tool. As such, the product development took a user-centric approach, involving those with journalism experience wherever possible.

The R&D process was structured and well-defined. This included a design probe workshop and user testing sessions, as well as more informal and continuous feedback. The project pulled together an editorial board of key influencers in the local media ecosystem, which included people from JOMEC (Cardiff University's School of Journalism, Media and Cultural Studies) and people with links to the media. Their task was to challenge the project and help meet journalists, editors, and others working in the industry. The project also built a user community of around 40 active journalists from across the industry, most of whom were from Cardiff. User group interaction took place through workshops and one-to-one conversations. These approaches uncovered what it's like to be a journalist, the problems they face, which mundane daily tasks take up valuable time, what tools they use, and what the pain points are. It indicated the possibility of creating a tool that would take some of those time-heavy elements away from journalists so that they could focus on information gathering and writing. These provided critical feedback and analysis on the usability of the platform and the information it contained.

The final part of the project allowed them to address some of this feedback, significantly altering the User Interface and connecting to new and different sources. Applying existing knowledge about AI and machine learning to a new context such as journalism was fundamental in exploring new possibilities that speed up the time it takes journalists to find reliable and relevant facts and sources.

The learning process was a consistent one, leading to four different user journeys and scenarios for product development. Each journey was scored on things like how commercial the idea is, how realistic the development roadmap is, and how closely aligned it is to what the company is already doing. The process helped to choose the most viable option for the next phase. Acquired knowledge and insight brought together new developments with AMPLYFI's existing capabilities in machine-learning, natural-language processing, User Interface, and backend processing infrastructure.

The entire learning process provided a better understanding of and deeper insight into the journalism sector. Moreover, the follow-up funding enabled the creation of a beta product representing an entirely new potential product for AMPLYFI in an entirely new sector. Learning how to prioritise research findings based on the key use case, while maintaining the rest of findings for future consideration, represented an important step in the research process. Gathering more information and data from journalists about their use cases helped to reinforce and further define many of the aspects of the beta version of the product development roadmap. Despite leaving areas for improvement, the project developed a functional tool that enables journalists to better interact with data and information.

3 ***Conceptualising innovation: Exploitative Learning Fuelling Open-Ended Exploration***
Conceptualising innovations represents a shift towards a more open-ended and exploratory approach to R&D. They break away from the structured framework, embracing a knowledge-based form of investigation that aligns with the concept of open innovation (Chesbrough, 2003). This openness allows for collaboration with external knowledge sources and the exploration of entirely new creative possibilities. However, unlike disruptive innovation (discussed below), conceptualising innovation relies heavily on exploitative learning, leveraging their existing knowledge base as a springboard for exploration.

Case study: Film Hub Wales

Film Hub Wales (FHW) supports organisations that screen films, with the aim of bringing the best British and international films to audiences across Wales and the whole UK. FHW is part of a UK-wide Film Audience Network, consisting of eight hubs funded by the British Film Institute. It leads the UK Inclusive Cinema strategy on behalf of the network. Their feasibility project, funded through Clwstwr, aimed to explore the idea of Welsh film branding. The main challenge addressed by the study was thus to see if it was possible to find ways of increasing awareness of the Welsh film industry by building a brand around it.

The R&D process behind the project was an open-ended and exploratory one. It involved collaboration with external specialists – such as, for example, a Wales-based research company, a university, and an arts centre. These provided both research expertise and practical knowledge and experience in topics such as brand testing and the exploration of identity perception. The R&D process was thus structured in parallel phases and involved a mix of methods designed to answer the research question.

The first stage involved researching perceptions of Welsh identity. The analysis of the research question also indicated the need to organise a workshop involving 20 screen industry partners (screen agencies, distributors, filmmakers, etc.) to find out how a Welsh film brand might support their organisations. Next, hired experts worked on brand perception issues. The devised method consisted of a focus group testing of artwork for the hypothetical brand by students. Finally, three case studies from international territories representing best practices in the film branding industry (Screen Ireland, Telefilm Canada, and the Swedish Film Institute) were identified and analysed. The mix of methods enabled work on the research question from multiple and complementary perspectives, which broadened the adopted perspectives and enriched the outcome of the feasibility study. An 80-page final report accompanied by an infographic stands as a testimony to the value of the research.

The learning base for the feasibility study relied much on external expertise. Therefore, new knowledge was acquired indirectly, through commissioned work, rather than representing first-hand experience. Leveraging the knowledge base of multiple areas of inquiry – research practice, branding, and identity perception – the feasibility study was able to not only compile an informed report but also provide deep knowledge and inspiring examples of how Welsh film branding could be more innovative. The mix of methods ensured a crossover of varied and complex sets of knowledge that fused into a comprehensive approach to building an innovative Welsh film brand identity. However, the learning process leveraged existing areas of knowledge without reflecting upon, questioning, or experimenting further with findings, like, for example, the case of exploratory learning.

4 ***Disruptive innovation: Pioneering New Knowledge through Open-Ended Exploration***

Disruptive innovation represents the most adventurous and unpredictable innovation within the creative industries. The R&D approach is characterised by high levels of uncertainty and a commitment to exploratory learning. Disruptive innovation embraces open innovation (Chesbrough, 2003) to its fullest extent, actively seeking out external knowledge sources and venturing into entirely new creative territories. This aligns with the concept of radical innovation (Anderson & Tushman, 2018), where innovation disrupts existing industry norms and potentially leads to paradigm shifts.

Case study: Monnow Media

Monnow Media is a media production company led by a freelance journalist that works on investigative journalism, production, editing, drone filming, and technology training. The project led by

Monnow Media and funded through Clwstwr aimed to explore radical new ways of doing journalism, one that does not operate top-down where journalists decide what people need to know, but rather bottom-up through audience perceptions and needs. By moving away from personalities and opinions and starting to present facts with context in an accessible, useful, and interesting way, the project explored innovative ways of presenting news.

The R&D process was open-ended and highly experimental. It combined multiple approaches and methods for reaching a model of presenting news in radically new ways. The iterative research process included: researching the concept of storytelling through a combination of literature review and interviews about storytelling as a way of connecting to audiences; exploring how journalistic values need to shift through a focus group with people from ethnic minorities; creating new building blocks for journalism by analysing collected data and identifying the main building blocks that need to shift in journalism (narrative structure, content, context, the agency of users, the tone of the writing, diversity, inclusion and transparency about how the news is made) and proposing a view of journalism that shifts these approaches; constructing seven working prototypes from the building blocks and testing these with over 1,200 users; refining the best prototype based on user feedback.

The freedom to design each research step based on the findings of the previous one, while also continuing to deepen and refine steps even after their development and revealing invisible links between these, was essential in setting up a flexible research process that represented a gateway to new possibilities in narrative journalism. The most successful prototype in user testing was the so-called newly developed 'narrative accordion' – a branching, collapsible way of telling stories online that went beyond the hierarchical, inverted pyramid format that journalists typically use (that puts the most important facts of news at the top with further news details then becoming gradually less important). The follow-up funding for the project explored how to overlay these new storytelling techniques onto artificial intelligence-based content creation models.

The learning process was steep and profound. The knowledge base built through the different research phases has generated a pool of expertise that has raised Monnow Media's profile. In addition, the project opened unexpected avenues for the Welsh journalism sector, putting Wales on the map of journalism innovation. In aligning with an open R&D model and an explorative learning process, the project ended up being something much deeper than expected, which explored the fundamental purpose of journalism and how to reach younger audiences, aligning fully with the purpose of radical innovation which is deeply transformative. The novel approach to presenting news asked questions and pulled apart the traditional inverted pyramid, forcing journalists to take a step back from how they write things and look at how to make news online engaging and meaningful in a playful and accessible way. As a result, the R&D process developed transformative ways of conducting journalism.

Conclusions

Our analysis has allowed us to develop a typology of R&D-driven innovation within the creative industries. This typology, built upon the direction of R&D and the depth of learning, sheds light on the diverse innovation journeys undertaken by creative businesses. Importantly, the framework identifies four distinct types of innovation: technocratic, incrementing, conceptualising, and disruptive. Recognising the value of each is crucial for fostering a multilateral and diversified innovation capacity within the creative industries.

Technocratic innovation provides stability and efficiency by addressing well-defined challenges. Incremental innovation offers progressive improvements and explores new applications for existing knowledge. Conceptualising innovation pushes boundaries and explores new creative forms, often leveraging existing knowledge as a springboard for the discovery of new creative endeavours. Disruptive innovation acts as a catalyst for radical change, venturing into uncharted territory and potentially revolutionising the creative landscape. We argue that the co-existence of these approaches ensures a balanced innovation ecosystem within the creative industries, fostering both refinement and exploration, as well as continuity and disruption. The developed framework offers possibilities for various stakeholders within the creative industries.

1 Creative businesses can utilise this framework to self-assess their desired innovation type and identify areas for improvement. By understanding their position on the spectrum, businesses can make informed decisions about resource allocation and collaboration strategies. For example, a business identified as aiming for a technocratic innovation might explore opportunities for open innovation to incorporate user feedback or explore entirely new creative territories.
2 Researchers can leverage this framework to deepen their understanding of innovation within the creative industries. The typology provides

a lens for analysing case studies and conducting comparative research across different creative industries sectors. Additionally, it can inform the development of new research questions and methodologies specifically tailored to the unique innovation landscape of the creative industries.

3 Policymakers can utilise this framework to develop more targeted support mechanisms for creative industries. By understanding the diverse R&D needs of different innovation types, policymakers can design support programmes that cater to the specific challenges and opportunities faced by technocratic, incremental, conceptualising, and disruptive innovation. This can include funding initiatives, skills development programmes, and infrastructure investments that nurture innovation across the entire spectrum.

This framework departs from traditional innovation frameworks that focus solely on the outcome of innovation, such as novelty or economic impact and therefore the often linear conception of novelty applied in policies and academia. By emphasising the R&D process itself, our framework offers several advantages. Firstly, it can be applied to a wider range of creative endeavours. Secondly, it is more helpful for policy frameworks as it allows for the design of support mechanisms that are not dependent on measurable and hard but decidedly blunt indicators. This is particularly relevant for the creative industries, where innovation often manifests in qualitative ways, such as the creation of new cultural experiences or the development of innovative storytelling techniques going beyond technological advancements. The framework presented here underscores the importance of valuing all types of innovation outputs and processes, not just those that lead to immediate commercial success. The exploration and experimentation undertaken by conceptualising and disruptive innovation forms can lay the groundwork for future breakthroughs and contribute to the long-term sustainability and vibrancy of the creative industries. Furthermore, the language applied in this new typology stems from research and case studies directly derived from the creative industries. While it still acknowledges research on innovation from various sectors, the emphasis on knowledge and learning in the framework makes it more accessible to creative industries stakeholders.

Finally, it is important to acknowledge the need for caution when designing support mechanisms for different innovation types. While fostering exploration and experimentation is essential, it is also important to ensure responsible use of resources and mitigate potential risks. The specific support offered to those practising disruptive innovation, for instance, might require a higher degree of flexibility and risk tolerance compared to the support provided to technocratic or incremental innovation. In summary, by acknowledging the full spectrum of innovation through the lens of R&D direction and depth of learning in the creative industries, this framework offers valuable insights for businesses, researchers, and policymakers.

References

Anderson, P., & Tushman, M. L. (2018). Technological discontinuities and dominant designs: A cyclical model of technological change. In *Organizational innovation* (pp. 373–402). London: Routledge.

Chandy, R. K., & Prabhu, J. C. (2010). Innovation typologies. In B. Bayus (Ed.), *Wiley international encyclopedia of marketing* (Vol. 5, pp. 1–9). Wiley. https://doi.org/10.1002/9781444316568.wiem05012

Chesbrough, H. W. (2003). *Open innovation: The new imperative for creating and profiting from technology*. Brighton: Harvard Business Press.

Cinar, E., Simms, C., Trott, P., & Demircioglu, M. A. (2024). Public sector innovation in context: A comparative study of innovation types. *Public Management Review*, *26*(1), 265–292.

Cohen, M. A., Eliashberg, J., & Ho, T. H. (2000). An analysis of several new product performance metrics. *Manufacturing & Service Operations Management*, *2*(4), 337–349.

Enkel, E., Gassmann, O., & Chesbrough, H. (2009). Open R&D and open innovation: Exploring the phenomenon. *R&D Management*, *39*(4),311–316.

Galindo-Rueda, F., & Verger, F. (2016). *OECD Taxonomy of Economic Activities Based on R&D Intensity* (OECD Science, Technology and Industry Working Papers 2016/04; OECD Science, Technology and Industry Working Papers, Vol. 2016/04). https://doi.org/10.1787/5jlv73sqqp8r-en

Garcia, R., & Calantone, R. (2002). A critical look at technological innovation typology and innovativeness terminology: A literature review. *Journal of Product Innovation Management: An International Publication of the Product Development & Management Association*, *19*(2), 110–132.

Gassmann, O., & Schweitzer, F. (Eds.). (2014). *Management of the fuzzy front end of innovation*. New York: Springer.

Gustafsson, C., & Lazzaro, E. (2021). The innovative response of cultural and creative industries to major European societal challenges: Toward a knowledge and competence base. *Sustainability*, *13*(23), 13267.

Hardy, C., & Dougherty, D. (1997). Powering product innovation. *European Management Journal*, *15*(1), 16–27.

Henderson, R. M., & Clark, K. B. (1990). Architectural innovation: The reconfiguration of existing product technologies and the failure of established firms. *Administrative Science Quarterly*, *35*(1), 9–30.

Knüpling, L., Wessendorf, C., & Basilico, S. (2022). Revisiting innovation typology: A systemic approach, Jena Economic Research Papers, No. 2022-002, Friedrich Schiller University Jena, Faculty of Economics and Business Administration, Jena.

Kovacs, A., Marullo, C., Verhoeven, D., & Van Looy, B. (2019). Radical, disruptive, discontinuous and breakthrough innovation: more of the same?. In S. Tanja (Ed.), *Academy of management proceedings* (Vol. 2019, No. 1). New York: Academy of Management.

Lichtenthaler, U. (2009). Absorptive capacity, environmental turbulence, and the complementarity of organizational learning processes. *Academy of Management Journal*, *52*(4), 822–846.

Lomas, E. (2017). *Defining R&D for the arts and knowledge cultural domains*. Research Report for Arts & Humanities Research Council (AHRC). University College London. https://discovery.ucl.ac.uk/id/eprint/1543295/1/R%26D_FinalReport_elomas_ahrc_ucl_2017.pdf

March, J. G. (1991). Exploration and exploitation in organizational learning. *Organization Science*, *2*, 71–87.

Miles, I., & Green, L. (2008). *Hidden innovation in the creative industries*. Project Report. NESTA. London. https://e-space.mmu.ac.uk/624532/

Oberländer, A. M., Stahl, B., Watkowski, L., Braadt, S., & Scherer, P. (2021). A two-sided approach for digital innovation at SCHOTT: Combining resource-and problem-oriented innovation methods for digital service development. In N. Urbach, M. Röglinger, K. Kautz, R. A. Alias, C. Saunders, & M. Wiener (Eds.), *Digitalization cases vol. 2: Mastering digital transformation for global business* (pp. 227–247). Cham: Springer Cham.

OECD. (2015). *Frascati manual 2015: Guidelines for collecting and reporting data on research and experimental development*. OECD. https://doi.org/10.1787/9789264239012-en

OECD & Eurostat. (2018). *Oslo manual 2018: Guidelines for collecting, reporting and using data on innovation*, 4th Edition. The measurement of scientific, technological and innovation activities. Paris/Eurostat. Luxembourg: OECD Publishing. https://doi.org/10.1787/9789264304604-en

Schartinger, D., Rehfeld, D., Weber, M., & Rhomberg, W. (2022). Green social innovation–towards a typology. In J. Terstriep, & D. Rehfeld (Eds.), *The economics of social innovation* (pp. 174–193). London: Routledge.

Snowball, J., Tarentaal, D. & Sapsed, J. (2022). Innovation and diversity in the digital cultural and creative industries. *Journal of Cultural Economics*, *1*(45), 705–733. https://doi.org/10.1007/s10824-021-09420-9

Van de Ven, A. H., & Ring, P. S. (2006). Relying on trust in cooperative inter-organizational relationships. In R. Bachmann, & A. Zaheer (Eds.), *Handbook of trust research* (pp. 144–164). Cheltenham: Edward Elgar Publishing.

Von Hippel, E. (2005). Democratizing innovation: The evolving phenomenon of user innovation. *Journal für Betriebswirtschaft*, *55*, 63–78.

Wölbling, A., Krämer, K., Buss, C. N., Dribbisch, K., LoBue, P., & Taherivand, A. (2012). Design thinking: An innovative concept for developing user-centered software. In A. Maedche, A. Botzenhardt, & L. Neer (Eds.), *Software for people: Fundamentals, trends and best practices* (pp. 121–136). Heidelberg: Springer Berlin.

4 Supporting R,D&I in the creative industries

Máté Miklos Fodor, Meiram Begentayev and Aliya Turegeldinova

Studying optimal levels and timing of R,D&I support

Gauging the right levels of support for R&D is a key part of cultivating an innovative environment in the creative industries, enabling innovative ecosystems to work as effectively as possible. The lack of understanding of R&D processes in the creative industries means there is little research about the optimal levels of R&D support (see also Chapters 1 and 2). The creative industries is a diverse sector consisting of project-based small enterprises, each with its unique demands and challenges (Flew & Cunningham, 2013). In previous chapters, we have described how, to address a range of different requirements, R&D support needs to be diverse and adaptable. Funding organisations can promote a more vibrant and varied innovation ecosystem by providing financial support for a wide range of creative projects (O'Connor & Gibson, 2015). Moreover, as we described in Chapter 1, the effectiveness of R&D support in the creative industries is heavily influenced by the available support, which often includes not only financial support but also opportunities to connect with networks, expertise, and spaces for collaboration (McRobbie, 2018).

In this chapter, we draw upon our analysis of R,D&I projects supported by the Clwstwr programme to address a very practical question: what are the optimal levels and timing of support for R,D&I projects? Our study examined 68 creative projects funded by Clwstwr. Data has been collected from project participants about their innovation journeys through thorough ex-post evaluations and interviews (see Chapter 1 for more information and details about the methodology). Our longitudinal method – asking projects to trace the success reached at various levels of their R&D journey in continuous time – acknowledges the dynamic nature of creative R,D&I and allows a better understanding of the intricate connection between support interactions and project satisfaction.

The findings highlight the importance of implementing a prompt and comprehensive support approach that is tailored to the specific needs of the creative industries. Funding schemes can enhance project satisfaction

DOI: 10.4324/9781003481805-4

This chapter has been made available under a CC BY-NC-ND 4.0 license.

and innovation outcomes by incentivising early milestones and maintaining moderate support engagement. The broader benefits of R&D assistance, such as increased resilience, innovation capacity, and socioeconomic spillover effects, underscore the significance of public investment for creative industries' R,D&I. We begin with a literature review about the current state-of-the-art in research on the effectiveness of public funding for R&D and the theoretical foundations of our analysis. The findings present a visualisation of the R&D journeys of creative industries' projects and the optimal support levels and timing.

Research on the effectiveness of public funding

The importance of public funding in promoting innovation has been widely recognised, particularly in industries where private investment is limited due to significant risks and uncertain profitability. Public funding can be obtained for innovation through various means, including grants, subsidies, tax incentives, incubator programmes, and collaborations between the public and private sectors. The effectiveness of these funding mechanisms is often contingent upon the way they are designed and implemented. Specifically, public funding has greatly benefited high-risk, high-reward ideas that may not attract private investment otherwise. An example of this is the Small Business Innovation Research (SBIR) programme in the US, which has granted funding to several emerging businesses that later become dominant players in the market, such as Qualcomm and Symantec (Wessner, 2008).

Addressing the 'valley of death' – the gap between the initial stages of development and market readiness – is a critical challenge in the field of innovation. Public funding has effectively addressed this gap by providing resources during the initial stages when private investment is restricted. Efforts like the European Union's Horizon 2020 have played a crucial role in assisting projects in overcoming this challenging phase, for example (Mazzucato, 2011). Public funding has facilitated the formation of alliances between the government, business, and academia, fostering collaborative innovation. According to Breznitz and Ornston (2013), these collaborations have played a vital role in promoting various sectors, such as biotechnology and renewable energy.

Despite these accomplishments, there are still several areas where the allocation of public funds for innovation has encountered challenges. In instances of bureaucratic inefficiency, partiality, and lack of transparency, funds may be assigned to projects that are deemed less deserving. This misallocation also diminishes the overall effectiveness of funding initiatives (Lerner, 2009). Another significant challenge is to ensure the ongoing viability of funded projects. Although public funding and support can stimulate innovation, sustained support or supplementary funding, which is not always guaranteed, is often necessary to ensure the long-term viability of these projects. Projects may experience a halt in progress once the initial funding period ends if they rely on public funding and lack a clear path to financial self-sufficiency (Azoulay et al., 2019). The effectiveness of public funding is also greatly affected by timing and organisation. Milestone-based funding, as described in the literature, can enhance accountability and focus by ensuring that payments are only disbursed upon the successful completion of specific project milestones. However, the task of selecting the appropriate benchmarks and schedule for these assessments remains challenging (Chen et al., 2020).

In terms of funding levels, inadequate support can lead to the failure of a project, while an excessive number of interventions (even if guided by the best intentions) can reduce the drive for creativity and effectiveness. So, for example, Gök and Edler (2012) advocate a balanced approach, which entails providing sufficient funding to meet project requirements without being overly generous and promoting wastefulness. In general, however, there is a lack of agreement on the optimal level of support for different types of projects, the most effective approach to organising funding to achieve maximum impact, and the appropriate timing for milestone reporting and achievements. These gaps indicate the need for evidence-based guidelines that can inform practices and policies regarding public funding. The theoretical foundation to analyse the optimal level and timing of funding for R,D&I includes various key concepts derived from organisational behaviour, economics, and innovation theory.

First, public funding has been – and remains – a key driver of innovation. From a macroeconomic standpoint, this is explained by public goods and market failure. The purpose of public funding is to address the market failure resulting from insufficient investment in R&D, especially in the creative industries. In these industries, the benefits of innovation are often non-rival and non-exclusive and difficult to achieve through private means (Arrow, 1972). Public funding is expected to generate significant positive externalities, such as knowledge spillovers and a more dynamic innovation ecosystem.

Second, resource-based theory posits that supporting resources play a crucial role in fostering innovation, particularly for small and medium-sized enterprises (SMEs) that often face constraints in funding (Barney, 1991). The provision of support can significantly enhance these businesses' ability to undertake and accomplish projects. However, there may be a point at which additional support does not yield proportional benefits, indicating diminishing returns. Similar observations also emerge from the absorptive capacity theory literature, which suggests that successful innovation is contingent upon an organisation's ability to recognise, assimilate, and utilise new knowledge (Cohen & Levinthal, 1990).

Third, organisational learning theory posits that achieving successful outcomes necessitates continuous learning and adaptation (Argyris & Schön, 1997). It is possible to attain an optimal level of engagement with funding programmes that will promote iterative learning and adaptation without hindering individuality or creativity. This supports the idea that projects that incorporate learning cycles and iterative feedback tend to achieve greater innovation outcomes and higher levels of satisfaction than projects that have either too much or too little external intervention.

Fourth, the stakeholder theory, proposed by Freeman (2010), highlights the importance of effectively managing relationships with all stakeholders in order to achieve organisational objectives. This suggests that interactions with funding organisations should be well-managed and should Align with expectations and interests of all parties involved. The hypothesis suggests that aligning the assistance received with the project will enhance project success and satisfaction, as it will be perceived as advantageous and collaborative.

Finally, according to the theory of planned behaviour (Ajzen, 1991), the expectations and satisfaction of participants play a crucial role in determining project outcomes. This theory highlights the influence of attitudes, subjective norms, and perceived behavioural control on shaping intentions and behaviours. So, for example, early project milestones will have a positive impact on participants' perceptions of control and progress. This, in turn, is expected to lead to increased overall satisfaction and project success. Conversely, decreased satisfaction can occur when milestones are achieved prematurely without adequate preparation, as this may be perceived as superficial advancement. The technology acceptance model (TAM) and innovation diffusion theory (Rogers, 2003; Davis, 1989) also suggest that the timing of milestones is crucial, albeit in different ways, as early achievements will validate the perceived usefulness and usability of the innovation, leading to greater acceptance and satisfaction.

Our theoretical framework therefore generates three testable hypotheses:

1 Optimising interaction with support teams can maximise project outcomes;
2 Achieving early milestones will enhance satisfaction and perceived control; and
3 Premature milestones and the associated expectations have a detrimental effect on the R&D process.

Understanding optimal support for R,D&I

Identifying the typical R&D journey in the creative industries

The data for this study were derived from two main datasets provided by 68 Clwstwr-funded projects. Both were collected ex-post, at the end of each project's life span (although many projects continued to develop after that point). During the data collection phase, representatives of projects were asked to trace their R,D&I journey visually, while also providing commentary at key moments in the timeline, including their project milestones. The project's lifespan has been split into four quarters, the length of which may be different from one project to the other: projects varied considerably in timelines, though most were between 3 to 12 months, while some received 2 rounds of support (seed funding and development funding – see Chapter 1). The project teams were also asked to characterise their expectations about their innovative processes before its start, as well as at its end. Scores, ranging from −2 to 2, were allocated to these distinct points in time, depending on the projects' characterisations of their expectations. Initial expectations reflect a baseline level of optimism for the R&D projects, while all other 'satisfaction' ratings (also ranging from −2 to +2) reflect how well these initial expectations had been met.

The visual ratings provided by the 68 projects for each project stage, when superimposed on one another, allowed us to visualise the 'typical' R&D journey in the creative industries (Figure 4.1). This is the 'typical' path in the sense that it provides the average score reflecting how well expectations have been met across all R,D&I projects. The summary statistics (with the corresponding standard errors) show relatively little spread (Table 4.1). A typical journey starts with high expectations, experiences a dip along the way but concludes on a high note, ultimately exceeding initial expectations.

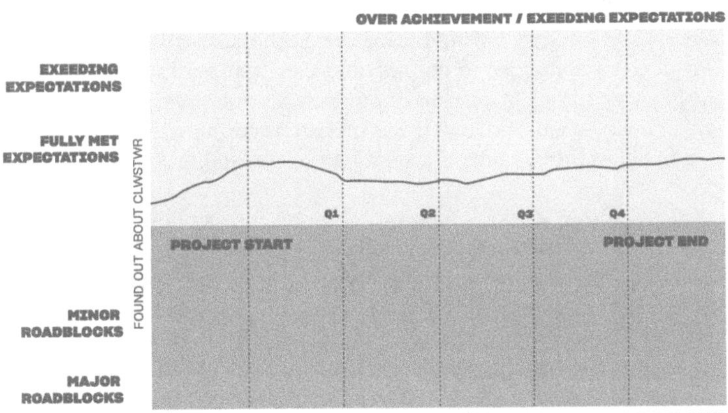

Figure 4.1 The typical R&D journey in the creative industries.

Table 4.1 Summary statistics of R&D journey in terms of expectations and how closely they have been met, on a scale from −2 to +2.

Time point	*Mean score*	*Standard error*
Initial expectations	0.3206	0.0243
End of pre-contract phase	0.7485	0.0302
End of Q1	0.5191	0.0211
End of Q2	0.5250	0.0234
End of Q3	0.5797	0.0229
End of Q4 (project end)	0.7059	0.0312
End of after-project period	0.7731	0.0337

The experience of the *Lewnah* project – which aimed to develop an engaging news programme for younger children – exemplifies a typical innovation journey and is useful to quote at length.

> So we signed the contract around September. We had no expectations really at all, having never undertaken R&D before, and doing a project that was out of our comfort zone. The project's about news which is our area, but we were using animation and technology that we were completely unfamiliar with. So I would say that we were thrilled, obviously, to get the initial bit of funding, which was seed funding, so we were kind of like up here. We didn't even really know where to start. The support that we got from Clwstwr was fantastic in terms of PDR workshops. They were incredibly helpful in giving us the initial tools of how to ask the right questions and get the right answers from the right demographics of people. I would say that from the off it kind of exceeded our expectations in terms of how much work there was to do and how possible and feasible it was because we were conducting this R&D alongside our day jobs as well. So, having exceeded expectations initially, I would say we probably continued to do that, and they were very supportive when we had some dips just in terms of our time. The only reason I put a slight dip in there was just because it was more time consuming than expected. I didn't have enough time to commit at various stages.

As well as satisfaction and expectation scores, milestones achieved have been documented and categorised. Milestones were aggregated by project and summarised by quarter, both before and after the project's end. The main milestones recorded are the following: (a) Commercial Readiness, (b) Hiring New Employees, (c) Increasing Turnover, (d) Increasing Exports, (e) Generating Revenue, (f) Developing R&D Strategy, (g) Spending Time on R&D, (h) Obtaining Intellectual Property (IP), (i) Societal Impact, (j) Environmental Impact, and (k) Partnerships. The milestones align with quantifiable measures in the KPI list used in the first part of the interview (see the methodology section in Chapter 1 for more details).

Table 4.2 The number of milestones reached at each stage of the innovation project on average across all projects participating in the research.

Period	*Mean milestones*	*Standard error*
Before project start	1.25	0.15
Quarter 1	2.75	0.21
Quarter 2	3.10	0.22
Quarter 3	2.60	0.20
Quarter 4	2.90	0.23
After project end	1.50	0.18

The summary statistics show how many of the above milestones have been reached across all projects on average (please note that there is no hierarchical ranking of milestones and each counts as 'one unit' in Table 4.2). The data suggests that milestone achievements peak in the 2nd and 4th quarters. Reading against the expectations timeline we can see that Quarter 3 comes at a time following a dip in expectations when projects were refining or refocusing their R&D projects. Post-project milestone achievement is lower, indicating that most significant milestones are planned and achieved within the project's active phase.

The optimal amount of support for R,D&I projects in the creative industries

We also collected data on how many times each individual project received support through the Clwstwr ecosystem. This included (a) interaction with support staff, (b) participation in training and workshops, and (c) participation in events (see Chapter 1 for more details). According to this definition, the average project has – during its lifespan within the programme – received support 4.28 times, with a standard error of 0.54. In line with the theoretical framework laid out in this chapter, two main hypotheses were examined with rudimentary econometric techniques. First, we examined the effect of the number of support sessions on the satisfaction scores at the end of the project (Quarter 4). The theoretical framework suggests that this relationship may be non-monotonic. To test if this is indeed the case, we ran the regression analysis (Equation 4.1).

Equation 4.1

Ordinary Least Squares regression to examine the optimal amount of support given to projects.

$$Y_i = a + b_1X_i + b_2X_i^2 + e_i$$

where Y_i is the project-specific satisfaction score about reaching expectations (between −2 and +2) at the project's end (Quarter 4), a is the constant term, b_1 and b_2 are regression coefficients reported in Table 4.3, X_i is the number of times that each project has interacted with Clwstwr and e_i is the project-specific prediction error. The theoretical framework, suggesting that there may be a 'sweet spot' for levels of support, would be confirmed if b_1 was statistically significantly positive and b_2 statistically significantly negative. If so, there would be empirical evidence that maximum satisfaction is reached at an intermediary level of support, while more extreme levels (either low or high) of support provide lesser satisfaction with the R&D journey.

The second hypothesis concerns the timing of milestones and satisfaction levels at the end of the project (as well as after the end), testing the theory that projects that hit milestones early generally report higher levels of satisfaction towards their end, but hitting them too early may be detrimental to long-term success. These hypotheses are evaluated using simple ordinary least squares regressions without quadratic terms as noted in Equation 4.2.

Equation 4.2

Ordinary Least Squares regression to examine the optimal timing of milestones.

$$Y_i = a + b_n X_{in} + e_i$$

where a is the constant term, b represents the regression coefficients, n is a number between 1 and 6, with 1 denoting the period before the projects signing the funding contracts and 6 the period after the end of the project. X_{in} shows the number of milestones reached by each project at stage n. e_i is the project-specific prediction error.

The first hypothesis on the optimality in the number of support interventions holds empirically (Figure 4.2). Average levels of satisfaction clearly increase in line with the number of interactions with the support to a 'sweet spot' of an optimal intervention rate, after which it decreases. This pattern is also documented in the regression output from running the regression in Equation 4.2 (Table 4.3).

The regression coefficients are as expected and very close to statistical significance. Since the sample is very small, the economic significance of the results is amplified. (It is very difficult to reach statistical significance at the 1, 5, or even 10% level with such small datasets, especially in the case of a non-monotonic regression.) Nonetheless, the evidence shown in Figure 4.2 is compelling enough to suggest that there may indeed be a 'sweet spot' in the number of interactions/interventions in R,D&I

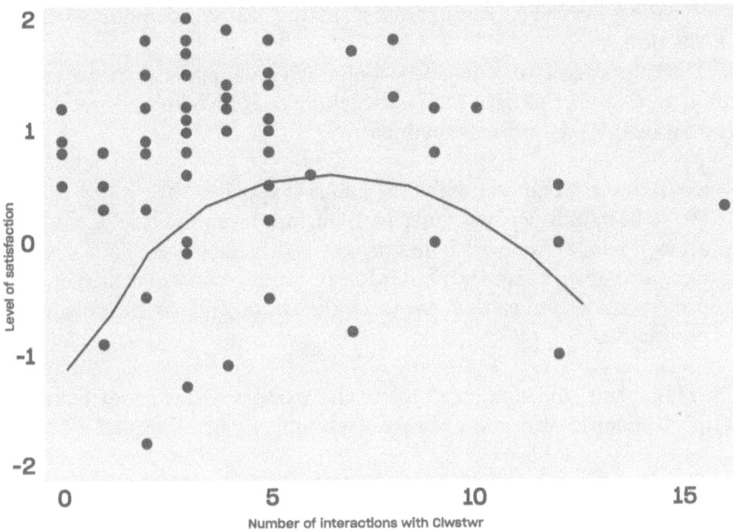

Figure 4.2 Scatterplot relating satisfaction levels reported by projects at the end of their R,D&I support (at the end of Quarter 4) and the number of interactions that they have had with the support provided.

Table 4.3 Regression output from running the specification in Equation 4.2.

		Regression coefficient	*Standard error*	*t-score*
Total support sessions with Clwstwr		0.132	0.099	1.34
Squared number of total support sessions with Clwstwr		−0.011	0.007	−1.56
Constant term		0.457	0.260	1.76
Number of observations	68			
R-squared	0.04			

projects. Projects that engaged at a moderate level showed higher satisfaction, supporting the idea that external support should enhance, not replace, internal capabilities. This finding highlights the importance of a balanced approach to support, where too much or too little interaction can be detrimental.

We should note, at this point, that the decrease in satisfaction associated with much higher levels of interaction may be a product of an attempt by the Clwstwr support team to 'rescue' or 'fix' projects that were encountering problems or difficulties. In other words, higher levels of intervention were a symptom rather than a cause of lower levels of satisfaction.

The importance of a balanced approach to support is expressed by Amplyfi, a project using AI to fast-track investigative journalism. As the lead on their R&D project explained:

> Clwstwr was great because it has put us in touch with so many people. We've been in touch ever since with our producer and it feels like they are still supportive even if the project is officially over. They (CO-Is) were also always very helpful and responsive. I think that the Clwstwr project made the relationship to Higher Education Institutions more productive.

The manager of the Aomame project also expresses the idea of balanced support, encapsulated in the phrase 'I got advice when I needed it':

> The Clwstwr team is brilliant, really supportive. I got advice when I needed it. You really felt they were behind you and rooting for you.

In terms of the timing of milestones reached, the results from running the specification in Equation 4.1 are provided in Table 4.4 below.

The only two regressions that are statistically significant are the number of milestones reached in Quarters 1 and 2 of the project. They imply that reaching one additional milestone in Quarter 1 of the project, holding all other things constant, decreases satisfaction at the end of the project by 4%. On the other hand, reaching one additional milestone in

Table 4.4 Regression output from running Equation 4.1 with the natural logarithm of satisfaction levels at the end of the project as the dependent variable.

		Regression coefficient	*Standard error*	*t-score*
Milestone reached before contract signature		−0.001	0.022	−0.06
Milestone reached in the 1st quarter of the project		−0.042	0.018	−2.31
Milestone reached in the 2nd quarter of the project		0.033	0.19	1.72
Milestone reached in the 3rd quarter of the project		−0.010	0.015	−0.65
Milestone reached in the 4th quarter of the project		0.013	0.017	0.78
Milestone reached after the end of the project		−0.022	0.013	−1.64
Constant term		1.36	0.08	16.05
Number of observations	68			
R-squared	0.14			

Quarter 2 of the project, holding all other things constant, increases satisfaction at the end of the project by 3%.

The theory of planned behaviour and innovation diffusion theory is supported by the importance of hitting milestones. Early achievements in Quarter 2 boost satisfaction, validating the project's direction and fostering a sense of progress. This aligns with the idea that perceived usefulness and ease of use are crucial for the adoption and success of innovations. Organisational learning theory is reflected in the negative impact of premature milestones. Early achievements may disrupt the iterative learning process, leading to reduced satisfaction. This underscores the need for a paced approach to innovation, allowing for continuous learning and adaptation.

The Goggleminds and the Democracy Box projects (which both had successful outcomes) are examples of the success of a well-paced R&D project. Goggleminds deployed VR to transform the healthcare education system. Throughout the two rounds of funding, the company progressed steadily through the research process. The manager of Goggleminds explained:

> I would say, we did hit some roadblocks quite early on, which was good in hindsight, because we were able to kind of rectify those. I wouldn't say the major ones (at the start), I would say sort of here (second quarter) and it kind of probably went like this for like a month or two (pointing at the graph). Because we thought initially that we solved it but actually didn't, someone else provided feedback on this and it's like: Oh OK, we didn't think about that. Actually what happened, towards the end is we built the platform, people were using it, and we were getting really, really good feedback, really good results. We could see actually what was happening was that we created something that people do find useful.

The Democracy Box project explored novel ways to develop democratic participation by co-creation with young people normally disengaged from politics. As the manager of the Democracy Box explained:

> The project allowed me to take my work into a different sector. I can't quite explain the impact of that. I didn't even know there was a democracy sector. It allowed me to research that, map that and create a bridge from the arts & cultural sector to democracy. I'm not pioneering that but I didn't know that I could do that. I am only just at the beginning of what that could become. If I do what I am trying to do now I am going to create a 12-month talking shop that would employ creative freelancers, as the hosts of it for a year or more and open satellite ones all over Wales. I will take other creatives with me into this other sector. What is really important is that their worth is really valued outside and in different sectors.

Conclusions

The findings from this analysis of R,D&I projects offer a data-driven perspective on how future public funding programmes can be strategically organised to optimise their impact on creative industries' innovation. The journey through funding allocation, support interaction, and milestone achievements reveals a number of lessons for successful creative industries' innovation ecosystems.

Firstly, the relationship between engagement with the support body and project satisfaction follows the 'Goldilocks' principle – not too much, not too little, but just right. Those who had either very regular or very infrequent interaction with the support personnel reported lower levels of satisfaction compared to those who maintained a reasonable degree of relationship. This indicates the existence of an optimal point where the desired outcomes are facilitated by the appropriate level of supportive engagement (Gong et al., 2013). Insufficient interaction can lead to a lack of guidance and support, while too much interaction may indicate too much reliance on others, hindering independent thinking and decision-making. It may be, as we have suggested, that higher levels of support were indicators of – rather than a cause of – projects less likely to succeed. Either way, it suggests that providing additional support in these instances has far less impact.

This finding challenges the model of hands-off funding, advocating an intervention strategy that provides critical guidance and support that enables projects to progress – without doing too much of the work for them. Once a project becomes too dependent on intervention and support, there is a law of diminishing returns in terms of time and resources spent. To provide the right level of interaction means offering guidance, feedback, and resources without compromising the autonomy of projects. This balanced engagement fosters a supportive environment where creativity and innovation can flourish organically, a system of 'smart support', allocating resources where they can make the most significant impact. This means providing enough support to empower innovation without fostering dependency or complacency.

Secondly, the timing of support emerges as a factor in project success. Our findings suggest that hitting milestones too early can be detrimental, as it may disrupt the natural learning and development processes inherent in R&D projects in the creative industries. Our regression analysis reveals a subtle connection between project satisfaction and the timing of milestone achievements. Projects that fulfilled targets relatively early were associated with higher satisfaction, suggesting that early successes can boost confidence and momentum (Edler et al., 2013). However, achieving these milestones too quickly may paradoxically lead to reduced satisfaction, as their rushed nature undermines the depth and quality of creative exploration. This highlights the importance of timing and pacing in the support process to achieve a balance between initial achievements and continuous growth. This may be a consequence of projects moving too quickly towards a specific solution, thereby closing off other (potentially more promising) avenues to explore. This indicates the value of strategic pacing – encouraging projects to achieve significant early milestones while allowing enough time for iterative learning, refinement, and potential changes in direction.

This suggests the need for funding strategies that prioritise medium-term innovative potential over short-term economic metrics in the creative industries' innovation ecosystem. By focusing on milestones that build intellectual capital and innovation capabilities, funding bodies can ensure that projects are more successful. Future programmes should embrace the inherent uncertainty and variability of R,D&I projects in the creative industries, offering tailored support that adapts to the unique needs and trajectories of each project and the sector. This approach not only ensures that a broader spectrum of R,D&I in the creative industries receives support but also fosters an environment where unconventional and high-risk projects can thrive. Inclusivity means recognising underrepresented innovation types (see also Chapter 3), ensuring that innovation is not just widespread but also diverse and equitable. This involves creating pathways for ongoing support, such as follow-up funding, continued mentorship, and robust networking opportunities (like Clwstwr aimed to establish). By doing so, funding bodies can help projects transition from public support to financial independence, ensuring that the initial investment generates lasting value and impact in R,D&I in the creative industries.

References

Ajzen, I. (1991). The theory of planned behavior. *Organizational Behavior and Human Decision Processes*, *50*(2), 179–211.

Argyris, C., & Schön, D. A. (1997). Organizational learning: A theory of action perspective. *Reis*, 1987(77/78), 345–348.

Arrow, K. J. (1972). *Economic welfare and the allocation of resources for invention* (pp. 219–236). UK: Macmillan Education.

Azoulay, P., Zivin, J. S. G., Li, D., & Sampat, B. N. (2019). Public R&D investments and private-sector patenting: Evidence from NIH funding rules. *Review of Economic Studies*, *86*(1), 117–152.

Barney, J. B. (1991). Firm resources and sustained competitive advantage. *Journal of Management*, *17*(1), 99–120.

Breznitz, D., & Ornston, D. (2013). The revolutionary power of peripheral agencies: Explaining radical policy innovation in Finland and Israel. *Comparative Political Studies*, 46(10), 1219–1244.

Chen, Y., Zhang, W., Yan, X., & Jin, J. (2020). The life-cycle influence mechanism of the determinants of financing performance: An empirical study of a Chinese crowdfunding platform. *Review of Managerial Science*, *14*, 287–309.

Cohen, W. M., & Levinthal, D. A. (1990). Absorptive capacity: A new perspective on learning and innovation. *Administrative Science Quarterly*, *35*(1), 128–152.

Davis, F. D. (1989). Perceived usefulness, perceived ease of use, and user acceptance of information technology. *MIS Quarterly*, *13*(3), 319–340.

Edler, J., Cunningham, P., Gök, A., & Shapira, P. (2013). Impacts of innovation policy: Synthesis and conclusions. Nesta Working Paper 13/21. https://media.nesta.org.uk/documents/impacts_of_innovation_policy_synthesis_and_conclusion_final.pdf

Flew, T., & Cunningham, S. (2013). Creative industries after the first decade of debate. In *Creative industries and urban development* (pp. 68–78). London: Routledge.

Freeman, R. E. (2010). *Strategic management: A stakeholder approach*. Cambridge: Cambridge University Press.

Gök, A., & Edler, J. (2012). The use of behavioural additionality evaluation in innovation policy making. *Research Evaluation*, *21*(4), 306–318.

Gong, Y., Kim, T. Y., Zhu, J., & Lee, D. R. (2013). A multilevel model of team goal orientation, information exchange, and creativity. *Academy of Management Journal*, *56*(3), 827–851.

Lerner, J. (2009). *Boulevard of broken dreams: Why public efforts to boost entrepreneurship and venture capital have failed—and what to do about it*. Princeton: Princeton University Press.

Mazzucato, M. (2011). The entrepreneurial state. *Soundings*, *49*(49), 131–142.

McRobbie, A. (2018). *Be creative: Making a living in the new culture industries*. Hoboken: John Wiley & Sons.

O'Connor, J., & Gibson, M. (2015). *Culture, creativity, cultural economy: A review*. Sydney: Australian Council of Learned Academies.

Rogers, E. M. (2003). *Diffusion of innovations*, 5th Edition. New York/London: Free Press.

Wessner, C. W. (2008). *An assessment of the SBIR program at the National Science Foundation*. Washington (DC): National Academies Press.

Conclusion

A roadmap for successful creative industries' R,D&I

Marlen Komorowski, Ruxandra Lupu, Justin Lewis and Máté Miklos Fodor

As we have discussed throughout this book, research, development and innovation (R,D&I) is a relatively new phenomenon in the creative industries. We are still learning how R,D&I is perceived and utilised, how it creates value and how it can enhance the ability of regional creative clusters – made up primarily of small businesses – to compete globally. In a broad sense, R,D&I is often equated with creativity and creative work but applying R,D&I in the creative industries is widely misunderstood. While creativity is crucial for innovation, R,D&I extends beyond imaginative thinking, involving a methodical and replicable approach to tackling real challenges and progressing from challenges to workable solutions. This book integrated four analytical dimensions – epistemological, perceptual, systemic and performative – to shed light on how R,D&I operates in the creative industries and how it can be effectively utilised to support a local innovation ecosystem.

Chapter 1 argues for rethinking rather than rejecting the idea of the creative economy, to allow economic structures to align with – rather than run counter to – cultural and creative value. We positioned our own work within that framework, arguing for the importance of an understanding of the creative economy and creative industries in order to develop new economic models to also produce positive social and cultural outcomes. The Clwstwr programme fits squarely within that model, aiming to create an ecosystem that supports the green, fair development of the creative industries, embracing place-making and positive social and economic impacts. The structure of Clwstwr – and its experimental and reflective approach to R&D – provides a strong and practical case for exploring the value and efficacy of R,D&I within the creative industries – one that goes beyond the techno-centric, linear, STEM-focused notions of R&D that have dominated both the literature and policy domains to date.

Chapter 2 presents our first analysis of the 68 Clwstwr R,D&I projects. It shows that a clear majority – 93% of respondents – found that while R&D often pushed them into unfamiliar areas, it was worth the

DOI: 10.4324/9781003481805-5

This chapter has been made available under a CC BY-NC-ND 4.0 license.

investment of time and resources. Even in traditional terms – using the typology of technology readiness levels – most Clwstwr projects achieved a level of progress that met their expectations. Despite the fairly modest levels of investment and limited time frames, over a third reached the later stages of readiness levels (developing a product, service or experience to a point close to market readiness). We further identified seven traits that characterise creative industries' R&D. Many of these – uncertainty, open-endedness, the need for learning, the discovery of new possibilities and so on – require time and resources, suggesting both the need for external funding and support systems to guide creative businesses through the complex terrain of R&D. This shows that although businesses in the creative industries find it challenging – associated with high levels of uncertainty – they recognise the importance and long-term impact of R&D.

Chapter 3 following on from Chapter 2, suggests a novel typology of R,D&I in the creative industries that is more accessible, inclusive and less focused on technology than most traditional models. This includes more experimental and less rigid approaches to conducting R&D, as well as acknowledging informal and flexible methods of transferring knowledge. This typology was based on the R&D processes the creative industries' projects go through to innovate, rather than stages between 'blue sky' and 'close to market' that define more traditional R&D processes. We developed a four-point grid based on two axes identifying the R&D process. The first axis describes the degree of pre-defined determination or R&D direction, from a highly focused and goal-oriented to a more open-ended and exploratory R&D process. The second axis describes the degree of learning throughout the R&D process, which ranges from refining existing knowledge and applying it to solve specific problems to acquiring new knowledge with the potential to open completely new (and hitherto unknown) opportunities. This gave us a framework identifying four different archetypes of creative industries innovation. (1) Technocratic innovation, which represents the most structured and focused form of innovation within the creative industries, and most closely aligns with traditional forms of R&D, where the primary goal is to refine existing knowledge and apply it to solve well-defined problems. (2) Incremental innovation, which also uses a structured R&D approach, while incorporating a degree of exploration within this framework, balanced between exploitative and exploratory learning. (3) Conceptualising innovation, which represents a shift towards a more open-ended and exploratory approach to R&D, embracing a knowledge-based form of investigation that aligns with the concept of open innovation. This openness allows for collaboration with external knowledge sources and the exploration of entirely new creative possibilities while leveraging their existing knowledge base as a springboard for exploration. (4) Disruptive innovation, which is characterised by high levels of uncertainty and a commitment to exploratory learning. Disruptive innovation embraces open innovation to its fullest extent, actively seeking out external knowledge sources and venturing into entirely new creative territories.

Chapter 4 looks into the optimal support levels for R,D&I projects in the creative industries. Clwstwr saw funding for R&D as part of a broader ecosystem – one that provided training in R&D methods (through UCD) and included a range of support and collaboration mechanisms. Our research endorses this approach and suggests that projects that engaged with this ecosystem of support were more likely to report successful outcomes than those that did not – although too much dependence could be counterproductive (for both the funding programme and the project). This indicates that innovation programmes that simply offer financial grants are less likely to be effective: essentially, Clwstwr's creation of an ecosystem and support network – in addition to funding – played a key role in its success.

As R&D activity in the creative industries' progresses, there will be a growing need for more sophisticated strategies, techniques and instruments to make the case for – and efficacy of – public investment. This research takes a significant step in this direction by offering a comprehensive roadmap for effective R,D&I in the creative industries.

Firstly, there is a need for an epistemic shift that aligns our understanding of value generation in the creative economy, fostering a model of innovation where economic targets align with forms of social and cultural value.

Secondly, it suggests an expanded conceptual model of R&D types and processes in the creative industries to understand the value and perception of R,D&I. Such a model should emerge, bottom-up, through creative businesses' own ideas about what effective R&D means in their sector, best developed during empirical, large-scale, 'action research' programmes such as Clwstwr. The model expands on existing models such as the one provided by the *Frascati Manual* by deepening our understanding of the concept both at the theoretical and practical levels in order to differentiate its practice from other sectors.

Thirdly, a model for classifying R&D-based typologies of innovation is useful for rendering the entire process of innovation within the creative industries more transparent. To date, much of the innovation work in this sector is associated with creativity and the ability to come up with new ideas. The proposed classification model expands on existing ones while distinguishing between different pathways leading to innovation and their particular operational specificities. In doing so, it sheds light on the variety of R&D pathways and mechanisms leading to innovation. It also provides a systemic overview of the innovation forms within the creative industries to guide practitioners and inform policymakers.

And fourthly, our book shows that we need more inclusive and flexible funding schemes that operate within a support ecosystem that should work for a sector based mainly on small businesses or freelancers with little capacity for R&D. These should not only provide seed funding, but a solid foundation that consolidates long-term resilience. Support schemes should take into account the need to incentivise early milestones and the need to maintain levels of engagement that support – but do not overly constrain – R&D. It should facilitate the building of inclusive funding schemes that embrace diversity and allow for the multiplicity of voices within creative industries to access R,D&I. It also needs to seek more long-term impact through follow-up funding, continued mentorship and robust networking opportunities while providing flexibility.

This book is one of the first systematic attempts – using quantitative and qualitative methods – to address the field of R,D&I in the creative industries. We hope the frameworks, models and instruments developed in this book form a coherent roadmap through which we can envisage how successful R,D&I can work in the creative industries. Overall, our work suggests that place-based R,D&I can add real social, economic and cultural value. There is clear evidence to continue supporting R,D&I in the creative industries through funding and support ecosystems, with levers and mechanisms that align to real industry needs and operate as effectively as possible to create long-term economic, cultural and social impact.

Appendix

Brief description of analysed Clwstwr projects

Company name: AGILE KINETIC
Description: *Interactive Design for Healthcare* is a project pursuing increased user engagement by making interactions with an orthopaedic surgery recovery app as user-friendly as possible for all patients.
Interview details (date and interviewee name): 11/02/2022, Peter Bishop

---

Company name: AMPLYFI
Description: *AI In the Newsroom* is a machine-learning-enabled platform that rapidly reads and analyses thousands of documents at a pace not humanly possible, enabling journalists to immediately get a digestible breakdown of complex topics and discover new angles and areas that are worth further investigation.
Interview details (date and interviewee name): 15/12/2021, Rony Seamons

---

Company name: AOMAME
Description: *Aomame.space* is an artist-themed online environment designed specifically for the artworld to host cultural content – an exploration of what art online looks like if it utilises existing technologies more imaginatively and avoids simply replicating the physical gallery experience.
Interview details (date and interviewee name): 07/10/2022, Ric Bower

---

Company name: BAIT
Description: *Production Management Platform* is a standardised production management platform for visual effects and motion design studios to allow collaborative and remote working.
Interview details (date and interviewee name): 08/12/2021, Peter Rogers

---

Company name: BOMBASTIC
Description: *Bombastic Digi platform* is a platform for creating and sharing interactive film sessions, with a focus on providing educational content for schools, helping teachers run classes that meet creative learning objectives.
Interview details (date and interviewee name): 10/12/2021, John Sean Tuan

---

Company name: BRIGHT BRANCH
Description: Bright Branch built a live interactive drama that the audience would be able to take part in from home, in real time.
Interview details (date and interviewee name): 29/11/2022, Jo Pearce

---

Company name: BRITTLE WITH RELICS
Description: *A People's History of Wales 1965–1995* is a project drawing on an extensive interview archive and exploring the use of audiovisual installations, large canvas projections and audio sculptures to tell the story of late 20th-century Wales.
Interview details (date and interviewee name): 12/02/2023, Richard King

---

Company name: BUMPYBOX
Description: Bumpybox looked at *Expanding IP and Brands through a virtual pipeline*. It made a linear broadcast pipeline into a more diverse, virtual 'brand pipeline' allowing the creation of more content for different platforms at a lower cost, while simultaneously working on series production.
Interview details (date and interviewee name): 02/02/2022, Sam Wright

---

Company name: BWLB
Description: The *Accordion* project developed functioning prototypes to allow podcasts to expand or contract to the listener's available time while maintaining structure, tone and listenability.
Interview details (date and interviewee name): 08/02/2022, Andy Taylor

---

Company name: CAERPHILLY
Description: *CaseFinder* is a software for Court lists and Registers that extracts and stores information in a searchable format to allow for effective planning.
Interview details (date and interviewee name): 22/04/2022, Richard Gurner

---

Company name: CAF
Description: The *CAF Climate Assembly* developed approaches to greening animation production, creating much-needed expertise in South Wales for a global industry.
Interview details (date and interviewee name): 01/11/2022, Lauren Orme

---

Company name: HYBRID NARRATIVE (Green Cymru Challenge Fund)
Description: Hybrid Narrative proposed a new approach to making films that transforms the amount of resources they require and their potential impact on the environment. It combined green screen filming with motion design techniques and low-cost digital tools to reimagine how we tell stories on screen.
Interview details (date and interviewee name): 11/11/2022, Chris Buxton

---

Company name: CONNECT TO CARE
Description: *Prompts* is an app that helps professional carers connect with the people they care for.
Interview details (date and interviewee name): 07/04/2022, Amy Taylor

---

Company name: CLOTH CAT ANIMATION
Description: The *Reinventing Animation Production with Game Engine Technology* project integrated game engine, real-time rendering within the animation pipeline.
Interview details (date and interviewee name): 08/08/2022, Jon Rennie

Company name: CORE
Description: *School News* is a regular news service pilot delivered to pupils within school hours, customisable by teachers to meet the needs of the curricula while creating a news habit among the next generation of viewers.
Interview details (date and interviewee name): 04/05/2022, Amanda Louise Richmond

Company name: CRIT+SPEC
Description: CRIT+SPEC built an app to improve workflow problems in the film and TV industry.
Interview details (date and interviewee name): 15/11/2022, Joelle Rumbelow

Company name: DEMOCRACY BOX
Description: For *The Democracy Box* project, Yvonne Murphy worked alongside 16–24 year olds, including those from low turnout constituencies, to co-create and curate new forms of engagement with democracy, to produce the prototype of an approach to civic engagement which can be developed and replicated across the UK.
Interview details (date and interviewee name): 14/12/2021, Yvonne Murphy

Company name: EDGE 21
Description: *Reel Reality* is an entertaining and engaging mobile platformfor sharing screen content and mapping Film and TV locations using a range of immersive technologies. The Reel Reality app connects audiences with content in real locations, combining the potential of AR/GeoAR interactivity, location information and screen content so the user can develop their own film/TV location experience and collect and curate content.
Interview details (date and interviewee name): 09/02/2022, Rebecca Hardy

Company name: EVOLVEMENT/EDGE 21

Description: The *Evolvement* project intelligently connects augmented reality (AR) with film or television programmes. It's an immersive story experience combining film with investigation gameplay. Players gather the evidence while watching the film then use that evidence to investigate, make deductions and close the case.

Interview details (date and interviewee name): 09/02/2022, Rebecca Hardy

---

Company name: FESTIVALS COMPANY

Description: The Festivals Company aimed to satisfy cinema audiences in a post-COVID world. It therefore explored how film festivals, like the Iris Prize, and exhibitors can balance in-person and online activity, creating an environment where audiences can feel engaged and included whether they are attending in-person or virtually.

Interview details (date and interviewee name): 28/10/2022, Grant Vidgen

---

Company name: FIELDWORK

Description: *From Here* is a project exploring the potential for transposing a live gallery experience through digital means to promote original artworks.

Interview details (date and interviewee name): 22/03/2022, Ceri Jones

---

Company name: FILM HUB WALES

Description: *Made in Wales* delivered a clear message for the digital generation to increase the awareness and appeal of Welsh screen content.

Interview details (date and interviewee name): 19/01/2022, Hanna Lewis

---

Company name: FOCUS SHIFT

Description: *Viewfinder for Sport* is a project which explored how to combine sporting heritage, tourism and AR/VR experiences to develop unique content that engages with the sports tourism market.

Interview details (date and interviewee name): 04/02/2022, Daniel Harris

---

Company name: FOR CARDIFF
Description: For Cardiff scoped the creation of a new bilingual tourism product that would use innovative digital and immersive technologies to showcase Cardiff's rich history and relationship with screen and help users explore the city.
Interview details (date and interviewee name): 22/02/2022, Carolyn Brownell

Company name: FRONTGRID
Description: Frontgrid used gamification and storytelling within ParadropVR flying experiences to nudge people to drive a greater understanding, care, appreciation and participation in their real-world environments.
Interview details (date and interviewee name): 01/12/2022, Tammy Ownes

Company name: GOGGLEMINDS
Description: Goggleminds explored the utility of immersive technology to deliver training to the healthcare sector. The project worked on the gamification and accessibility of a training simulation using virtual reality (VR) to train healthcare professionals. The project aimed to give organisations better access to high-quality training content, improving efficiencies and flexibility.
Interview details (date and interviewee name): 22/07/2022, Azize Naji

Company name: GOOD GATE MEDIA
Description: The *Real Time Rendering and Interactive Promo* project developed a piece of IP into an interactive movie. It used an adaptation of Ian Livingstone's book, Deathtrap Dungeon, where it mixed high-end VFX with real-time computer rendering to greatly lower production costs by building photoreal sets within a computer as opposed to using physical artefacts.
Interview details (date and interviewee name): 16/12/2020, John Giwa Amu

Company name: GOLWG
Description: *Fôtio am Fory* is a project operating on the democracy section of the Golwg360 news website and targeting young people who are voting for the first time.
Interview details (date and interviewee name): 05/05/2022, Owain Schiavone

Company name: GORILLA
Description: Gorilla developed a new toolkit for post-production editing for remote work that enabled teams operating from different locations to work on the same material without the need for physical travel.
Interview details (date and interviewee name): 23/03/2022, Rich Moss

Company name: GREEN GATHERING
Description: *Beyond the Festival* is a unique online festival experience researching the use of innovative screen-based technologies to effectively engage wider audiences with environmental, sustainability and climate change issues in order to inspire sustainable lifestyle changes.
Interview details (date and interviewee name): 08/11/2022, Steve Muggeridge

Company name: HERITAGE WALKERS
Description: Heritage Walkers developed a proof of concept for a digital learning experience in partnership with the National Slate Museum.
Interview details (date and interviewee name): 01/08/2022, Carrie Westwater

Company name: HISSING CURRENTS
Description: Hissing Currents reimagined the music concert experience and album release cycle by creating an immersive storytelling experience through new technology in flexible spaces, while challenging recording industry norms about the album form.
Interview details (date and interviewee name): 20/01/2023, Gruff Rhys

Company name: HIDDEN NARRATIVES
Description: Hidden Narratives developed an *Interactive Documentary Format* that explored the role of content, format, marketing and distribution of interactive documentaries to reach a wider audience and become a viable career for producers.
Interview details (date and interviewee name): 14/04/2022, Nerys Wyn Evans

---

Company name: HIJIN
Description: *Inclusive Film* explored how screen content could be made in an authentically inclusive way for learning-disabled and/or autistic (LD/A) actors, and what new processes might be needed to create inclusive storytelling.
Interview details (date and interviewee name): 09/12/2022, Dan McGowan

---

Company name: CANDYLION
Description: Candylion explored the possibilities of making an animated feature film and a game at the same time using the Candylion design artwork across both platforms, to potentially streamline costs, maximise efficiency, broaden reach and exploit the innovation in both the process and technology in an international, commercial context.
Interview details (date and interviewee name): 25/01/2022, Catryn Ramasut

---

Company name: IUNGO
Description: Iungo developed a careers management platform for aspiring creative freelancers. It aimed to engage, inspire and inform new, returning and early career freelancers; helping them to grow their confidence, connections and professional capabilities.
Interview details (date and interviewee name): 27/01/2022, Jessica Leigh Jones

---

Company name: JONATHAN DUNN
Description: *Variations through Editing* is a project establishing deep collaboration with the blind/visually impaired community to understand current lived experiences. The result is an interactive tool generating a personalised variation of a dance film – a unique edit collected from a shared library of footage.
Interview details (date and interviewee name): 18/08/2022, Jonathan Dunn

---

Company name: JOANNA WRIGHT/KATE LAWRENCE
Description: The *Invisible Light* project explored how access for blind and visually impaired people can be built into the creation process of live performance and creative digital work, rather than delivered in post-production, to contribute to the experience of all audiences.
Interview details (date and interviewee name): 22/03/2022, Joanna Wright, Kate Lawrence

---

Company name: LAKU NEG
Description: *Laku Library* is a platform to gather and share African diaspora and indigenous stories on screen. This project aimed to better understand – through a series of interview prototypes – the ways in which care and agency can be interwoven in life storytelling, paying particular attention to form, content and sustainability.
Interview details (date and interviewee name): 24/01/2022, **Adeola** Dewis

---

Company name: LEWNAH
Description: *Kids News* is a technical prototype of an engaging children's news show combining animation and news footage.
Interview details (date and interviewee name): 21/10/2022, Hannah Vaughan Jones

---

Company name: LITERATURE WALES
Description: *Welsh Lands and Lore* is a Video Game Adaptation of Land of Legends. The project analysed the commercial viability of new video game content based on Welsh myths and legends, exploring the demand for new assets – artworks, animations, retellings – developed by Welsh writers, artists and game developers.
Interview details (date and interviewee name): 02/03/2022, Owen Wyn Jones

---

Company name: LITTLE BIRD
Description: *Green Screen* explored ways to help production companies across Wales make the media production process as environmentally sustainable as possible.
Interview details (date and interviewee name): 11/08/2022, Nida Harwood

---

Company name: MARTHA STONE
Description: *Life Lab* is a socially transformative story-based game addressing the impact of Adverse Childhood Experiences (ACEs) to explore online what a trauma-informed, resilient community could look like.
Interview details (date and interviewee name) 21/09/2022, Bryn Roberts, Suzanne Phillips

---

Company name: MAPPED OUT
Description: *Delivering News to Visual Thinkers* researched and developed a prototype of news that can be delivered to a more neurodiverse audience, making mainstream news more accessible and inclusive with a focus on visual thinkers.
Interview details (date and interviewee name): 17/03/2022, Linus Harrison

---

Company name: MISSION DIGITAL
Description: *Origami* is a prototype that proves the viability of a fast, simple, easy-to-use web app-based SAAS. It automates the delivery of files from where they are located to where they are needed, in the necessary video format and includes rich metadata for VFX and post-production in high-end TV and film.
Interview details (date and interviewee name): 23/02/2022, Tom Rogers

---

Company name: MONNOW MEDIA
Description: *News Storytelling through Modular Journalism* created and tested new and imaginative storytelling techniques with the aim of using innovative content management technology to build stories that reimagine how news might be presented to different audiences. Working with BBC News Labs and academics, Shirish Kulkarni used developments in "modular" journalism to explore how stories can be told most effectively, created most efficiently and understood more comprehensively.
Interview details (date and interviewee name): 16/08/2022, Shirish Kulkarni

---

Company name: NDC WALES
Description: *Moving Layers* ideated and tested new ways to make and experience dance using layered-reality technologies, prototyping an experience that enables a diversity of people to witness and participate in dance stories that change the audience/ performer relationship and connect people to their own physicality.
Interview details (date and interviewee name): 01/02/2022, Paul Kaynes

---

Company name: NIMBLE
Description: *Women's Football Content Hub* ideated and tested the world's first digital and social hub for women's football content – a platform to promote, discuss and drive this exponentially growing community.
Interview details (date and interviewee name): 13/01/2022, Katy Cartwright

---

Company name: OBJECT MATRIX
Description: *IMAGE VISION* combined a set of video asset management tools, together with a unique framework, to enable multiple algorithms to be incorporated for intelligent search. It unlocked video archives with search tools so that clips and videos can be brought to the operator's attention using a deep level of intelligence while incorporating (much as an iPhone app store can) algorithms for search and analysis that come from a local hub of developers.
Interview details (date and interviewee name): 25/05/2022, Jonathan Morgan

---

Company name: PAINTING PRACTICE
Description: *Plan V* is a virtual reality (VR) bespoke studio environment which can be used directly through a local and/or remote framework, allowing the user to experiment with lenses, storyboards, pre-visualisation and many other options. It represents a new step between script writing and the physical set building, reducing costs while increasing production efficiency.
Interview details (date and interviewee name): 12/08/2022, Yassmine Najime

---

Company name: JONATHAN CAMPBELL
Description: *Placemaker* investigated how screen-based media might enable people to better engage with their built surroundings and meaningfully contribute to its design.
Interview details (date and interviewee name): 10/01/2022, Jonathan Campbell

---

Company name: RESCAPE
Description: The project developed by Rescape deployed VR to transform childbirth. Building on their work and learning with midwives, Rescape created and tested specific therapies and educational content to help mothers-to-be during labour.
Interview details (date and interviewee name): 28/01/2022, Kevin Moss

---

Company name: SCREEN STREAMER
Description: Screen Streamer developed a web-browser-based service for recording, sharing and streaming your screen that offers a real-time one-to-one screen-sharing call feature and incorporates multiple-party sessions. The solution researched and developed longer recording times, increased storage space and new recording.
Interview details (date and interviewee name): 24/02/2022, Richard Morgan

---

Company name: SEVERN SCREEN
Description: Severn Screen developed a sustainable and collaborative infrastructure model to support the future of film and TV production. The process combined carbon footprint analysis with reporting on sustainability success stories and concept development for new apps/platforms.
Interview details (date and interviewee name): 01/08/2022, Mathew Talfan

Company name: SMALL AND CLEVER
Description: The *Virtual Production for Comedy* project improved the quality, reliability and ease of use of virtual production (VP) techniques, to enable VP as a standard tool for short-form comedy makers and other genres.
Interview details (date and interviewee name): 18/05/2022, Phillip Moss

Company name: SR IMMERSIVE
Description: SR Immersive developed a variety of offerings to suit the changing needs of clients and audiences, integrating emerging technologies such as VR and XR with traditional theatrical techniques, to create experiences that blur the line between real and virtual.
Interview details (date and interviewee name): 01/10/2022, Matthew Dunford

Company name: SUGAR CREATIVE
Description: *Project V* is a VR Storytelling Platform with a next-gen story engine for the creation of VR experiences from both new and existing narrative content. It represents a combined modular tool for the development of story structure and the efficient creation of interactive VR narrative experiences, allowing holders of IPs to work creatively to generate immersive interactive versions of the content.
Interview details (date and interviewee name): 24/11/2022, Will Humphrey

Company name: WHITE TENT COMPANY
Description: The *AR Murder Mystery* project explored AR and VR technology's potential to enhance the quality and immersive nature of the murder mystery experience.
Interview details (date and interviewee name): 27/02/2022, Cherry Barber-Mansell

---

Company name: GRACE QUANTOCK
Description: The *Trauma Toggle* project combined real-world clinical experience with journalists working in the field, marginalised audiences and technological developers to create a new prototype that is trauma informed. The Trauma Toggle allows users to titrate language and triggering material to control their media consumption.
Interview details (date and interviewee name): 28/07/2022, Grace Quantock

---

Company name: TREDBOY PICTURES
Description: The *Micro-Form Drama Across Multiple Platforms* project researched and developed the creation of a platform enabling users to bring together the different storytelling elements of various social media platforms to create joined-up stories on one dedicated app.
Interview details (date and interviewee name): 30/03/2022, Robert Morgans Evans

---

Company name: TRIONGL
Description: Triongl explored the possibility of making back-to-back bilingual or multilingual television dramas that export Welsh expertise to potential partners in Europe and beyond.
Interview details (date and interviewee name): 30/08/2022, Alec Spiteri, Nora Ostler Spiteri

Company name: TUNNEL VISION

Description: Tunnel Vision explored how new and emerging technologies can enhance the public transport passenger experience, through the delivery of audio, video and text content that is geospatially and contextually aware of passengers' needs.

Interview details (date and interviewee name): 13/03/2022, Pat Younge

---

Company name: VICKI APPLETON

Description: *Divergent Emergent* is a project aiming to bridge the employment gap for neurodivergent and disabled people through research and development of a neuro-inclusive and accessible application, creating multimedia access documents which enable users to talk about their strengths and skills, use their authentic 'voices' to communicate what their needs are and helping businesses be the best equipped they can be to meet needs from their first interactions.

Interview details (date and interviewee name): 14/01/2022, Vicki Appleton

---

Company name: VOICE WALES

Description: The *Photo agency* project addressed a significant lack of quality images that document the people and politics of Wales by researching and developing a ground-breaking photo agency for the Welsh news industry.

Interview details (date and interviewee name) 13/04/2022, Faith Rhiannon Clarke

---

Company name: YPOD

Description: The *Smart Podcasts* project developed functioning prototypes to allow podcasts to expand or contract to the listener's available time while maintaining structure, tone and listenability.

Interview details (date and interviewee name): 16/02/2022, Andy Taylor

Company name: WALES INTERACTIVE
Description: The *Interactive Movie HUB* project explored new pipelines and applications for creating and distributing interactive movies worldwide, making them more accessible and expanding the possible audience exponentially.
Interview details (date and interviewee name): 30/05/2022, Rich Pring

---

Company name: YELLO BRICK
Description: Yello Brick explored geolocated fragmented storytelling as a new way of telling stories in physical and digital spaces. The company created fragmented narratives that enabled audiences to have agency within the story experience, challenging traditional formats and developing new ones.
Interview details (date and interviewee name): 15/08/2022, Allie John

---

Company name: 73 DEGREE FILMS
Description: 73 DEGREE FILMS explored the potential of vertical video and its multifunctionality. To test out different potential ways of using the vertical films, four versions of the same three films were created. One would be viewed in a virtual reality headset, one inside a bespoke mobile application using novel gestures, one via an interactive display and one via a television.
Interview details (date and interviewee name): 21/11/2022, Robert Corcoran

Index

FSC
www.fsc.org
MIX
Papier | Fördert gute Waldnutzung
FSC® C083411

Kolibri 360 GmbH
Ferdinand-Jühlke-Straße 7
99095 Erfurt, Deutschland
produktsicherheit@kolibri360.de